BOOKS *about* BOOKS

ROADS
TO READING

Ralph C. Staiger

unesco

Published in 1979
by the United Nations Educational,
Scientific and Cultural Organization,
7 Place de Fontenoy, 75700 Paris
Printed by Presses Universitaires de France,
Vendôme

ISBN 92-3-101642-3
French edition: 92-3-201642-7
Spanish edition: 92-3-301642-0

© Unesco 1979
Printed in France

Preface

Promoting the reading habit has long been a major theme of Unesco's Book Development Programme. Although statistics on the world's illiterate populations are relatively easy to obtain, little is known about the millions of literate adults who rarely pick up a book or open a magazine, or about schoolchildren for whom reading has come to mean textbooks and little else.

The causes of this phenomenon are still the more difficult to determine because there is not one kind but many kinds of reading, and because reading habits vary considerably according to age group, educational level and socio-cultural background. Reading research, a relatively young branch of science, has provided clues to the significance of reading, both for the individual and society, but much ground remains to be explored if non-readers are one day to become readers.

The present publication is an attempt to report on various practical methods adopted throughout the world to promote and develop the reading habit among those literate populations that read little or nothing at all. The countries surveyed represent the major geographic regions of the world and illustrate a broad variety of internal structures. For example, leading publishing giants are looked at as well as countries where indigenous publishing is in its earliest stages; highly literate societies are considered as are those which have recently embarked on the path to literacy; monolingual countries and multilingual cultures are both represented here. Yet despite these disparities one common thread emerges: no country is satisfied with the number of active readers it counts among its population and all consider that methods and techniques for

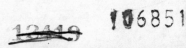

increasing reading must be tried and tried again in order to bring books and people together in a lasting and fruitful relationship.

While this book is in no way exhaustive, it may, it is hoped, provide helpful ideas and guidance for teachers, administrators and book professionals dedicated to devising and planning large-scale reading promotion campaigns. It reflects the results of Mr Staiger's considerable research as well as his own thinking based upon long professional experience as Executive Director of the International Reading Association. Although his views do not necessarily reflect those of Unesco, the Organization considers that this study is a timely and productive contribution to the cause of books and reading.

Contents

Contents

Foreword

The reading habit is an acquired one, as are most habits. It is regarded as desirable by most educated people, a habit which has a positive influence on an individual and a nation.

This book is a collection of ideas that have been used in many countries for the encouragement of reading. It may be considered as a source of ideas for campaigns to promote the reading habit. Its purpose is threefold: to provide information about reading and the reading habit as a foundation for action; to put forward examples of local, national and international reading promotion activities selected as useful, representative of different approaches, and adaptable to other places; and, finally, to suggest ways in which groups and individuals can proceed to encourage others to contract the reading habit.

The book is not a blueprint for reading promotion programmes in all countries, or in any one country, for it is suggestive rather than prescriptive. If a scheme appears to be worthy of imitation, adaptation may be in order; it is usually not desirable to borrow any programme *in toto* without change.

It should be clear that a person must have some competence in reading before a reading habit can be formed. The programmes discussed are designed to encourage already literate individuals to achieve a higher literacy; they are not a part of adult literacy or remedial reading programmes except as they are a part of a plan for continued lifelong education. This book is concerned with adequate readers who are competent to read far more than they do. It is for these readers who can read, but do not, that reading promotion campaigns are planned.

Some of the co-operating individuals from the various countries represented to whom deep gratitude is due are:

Singapore: Hedwig Anuar, National Book Development Council, National Library.

United Republic of Tanzania: S. R. Sijaona, National Commission for Unesco, Ministry of Education.

Japan: Sakiko Kurasawa, Noma Institute of Educational Research.

Canada: Robin Jackson, Office of the Secretary of State, Ottawa.

Brazil: Propicio Machado Alves, Livros Técnicos e Cientificos Editora, who is also President-elect of the International Publishers Association, and Ezequiel Theodora da Silva of Unicamp, São Paulo.

Federal Republic of Germany: Sigfred Taubert, former director of the Frankfurt Book Fair; and Hans Halbey, Director of the Gutenberg Museum, Mainz, also President of the International Board of Books for Young Children.

Australia: Michael G. Zifcak, Chairman of the National Book Council in Melbourne.

Austria: Gerhard Prosser. Austrian Booksellers Association, Richard Bamberger, Austrian Bookclub for Children, and Otto Georg Prachner, booksellers.

New Zealand: Kate Fortune, New Zealand Book Council, D. J. Heap, Heinemann Educational Book, and Roger Hewitson, Freyberg High School.

Republic of Korea: Byongwon Kim, Korean Institute for Research in the Behavioural Sciences, Seoul.

Hungary: István Kamarás of the National Szécheny Library, Budapest.

United Kingdom: Martyn Goff, National Book League, London.

United States: Paula Quint, Children's Book Council, New York, N.Y.

The members of the International Book Committee provided inspiration and useful details. National affiliate presidents of the International Reading Association are also due grateful thanks for providing accounts of activities in their countries.

Finally, to Gloria Smith, librarian at the association's headquarters, and Pat Balthis, who typed the manuscript, thanks for help beyond the call of duty.

Part 1

THE BACKGROUND

How we read

Some people have developed the habit of reading books. And some have not. Among the latter, many have learned to read, but do not. Perhaps they should be called 'lapsed readers'.

'Lapsed readers' are of great concern to many members of the book world, who see talents going to waste. This concern is not a selfish one, for the dedicated reader enjoys his habit, enlarges his world through his reading and regrets seeing others not using their gifts.

A child who is starting to learn to read has not yet developed the habit of reading. He may be taking a first step in that direction, but whether he will become an avid reader or a lapsed reader is a question which cannot be answered. In all probability, he will be neither, but will fall some place between these two extremes.

Skill in an activity is basic to enjoying it. The child who does not run well and is physically clumsy and maladroit is not likely to seek a place in a football team. Indeed, he probably will find every excuse to avoid playing football.

Desire and aptitude are not the only factors involved in developing a habit, of course. Time is also involved, for habits grow over a period of days, months and years. The automatic response of a habit can come only with long practice.

Many influences promote or deter the development of the reading habit. They are sometimes subtle and often interrelated, and are not always straightforward or evident on the surface. Although observers may be tempted to assign a single determinate, depending upon their biases or vantage points, no single cause is usually clear. The next chapter will discuss these influences at length and in more detailed fashion. This chapter will deal with how the reading act is developed.

WHAT IS READING?

It has only been during the last hundred years that the mechanics of reading have been systematically observed, and from this observation some specific knowledge has been gained about the nature of the reading process. Although some ancient and medieval writers commented with great insight on the nature of reading, their remarks were not the result of systematic observation. It should be kept in mind that the nature of the reading which they discussed was pre-Gutenberg, before the spread of knowledge, and long before the book revolution.

Most research in reading has been conducted with children as they are learning to read, but the earliest studies were done with adult subjects. We know through observation and eye-movement photography that adult reading is performed with saccadic, or jumpy, movements and short fixation pauses rather than in sweeping eye movements across the page. The number of words or letters recognized during the fixation pause appears to be related to intelligence, to the reader's familiarity with the subject, and to the difficulty encountered in the recognition of words or assimilation of ideas, as well as the physical features of the material being read, the syntax and the clarity of the writing style. Even with these varied influences upon him, a reader tends to develop ocular-motor habits which persist in many reading situations.

The chief value of photographing eye movements has been that they reflect, to a limited extent, what is happening as the brain comprehends what is seen. If an error, or miscue, is made, the eyes reflect the concern of the reader as he returns to the beginning of the line, or to another point of confusion. From eye-movement photographs, we can often predict the silent or oral reading patterns of a subject.

The mass of research studies on teaching children to read extend from the nineteenth century to the present; they have often been the subject of unnecessary emotional controversy.

All the facts are still not available, but this has not prevented many people from developing simplistic explanations of how children learn to read. One world-wide methodological controversy is that which surrounds the 'global' versus the 'analytic' methods of developing word recognition. Each 'method' has its proponents and in some countries, this controversy has raged periodically for over a hundred years. Usually disregarded are the findings of a series of studies [1][1] that indicated that no one method is superior in all cases, but that the adaptation of the materials used to the learner's needs, and the teacher's faith in the efficacy of a method are overwhelming factors in the pupil's success.

The reading process is still being actively studied through research. A comprehensive collection of research studies which reveals many of the concerns of scholars, and reproduces some of the classic studies has been compiled by Singer and Ruddell [2]. It shows that the concerns are: language acquisition and complexity, visual processing, perception, word recognition, cognition, affect, cultural interaction and teaching. It is not our purpose here to be exhaustive on this subject. For the reader who wishes to pursue the matter at greater length, many books are available on the subject.

READING IN DIFFERENT LANGUAGES

The influence of various languages upon reading has often been discussed. Differences in the reading process and in purposes for reading in many languages were studied by Gray in preparation for his volume, *The Teaching of Reading and Writing* [3]. By studying the eye movements of mature readers from fourteen different countries, he found that the eye-movement records supplied striking evidence that the basic processes used in reading Arabic, Burmese, Chinese, English, French, Hebrew, Hindi, Japanese, Korean, Navaho, Spanish, Thai, Urdu and Yoruba were similar, independent of the language read, its structure, or the kinds of characters or letters

1. The figures in brackets refer to the references at the end of this chapter.

used. Most words were perceived instantly as wholes, often in groups of two or three words, as the eyes progressed. When a new or difficult word was met, the good reader hesitated and attempted to analyse it. Good readers in all languages read more rapidly silently than orally. It is interesting to note that at the time Gray was preparing to do his study, consultants from many countries insisted that the habits and skills of reading varied with the form and structure of the language. His data did not bear out their beliefs.

SPEED OF READING

The press of print which seems to overwhelm us had added luster to the idea of reading quickly and has contributed to the growing desire on the part of many intelligent adults to improve their reading speed. Commercial courses are being offered in many places, and some advertisements for speed reading programmes border on the deceptive. Some promise results which cannot be achieved. Others provide testimonials which suggest that great men have profited from the course. Rarely do they indicate that only some especially endowed students—and not everyone who takes the course—achieve superior results. Furthermore, the bilingual reader is at a disadvantage when the language being read is not his mother tongue, and this is not mentioned in the advertising. It is obvious that an individual who is not at ease with a language is likely to encounter difficulty when he starts taking short cuts with the written form of that language.

This does not mean that individuals should not try to improve their rate of reading. Indeed, many readers are limited by a slow, word-by-word approach to print and can easily develop a variable-rate approach to reading in a familiar language.

One of the accepted short cuts is skimming—gaining an author's intent or identifying the important ideas in a selection. Each word is not read, but the reader skims over the surface of the material with full knowledge that some aspects may be missed.

Scanning is a name given to a technique which most good

readers use often. It may be defined as skimming with a specific purpose. As one searches for a name in a telephone book, or a word in the dictionary, each word is not read. We have learned to disregard the unrelated, unwanted words as we pursue our goal—the telephone number, or the word in the dictionary—for which our scanning is being done.

One danger which faces the neophyte is that of equating rapid reading, skimming and scanning with studying. They are not the same, except perhaps for a few individuals who have an unusual form of 'photographic' memory. Neither should the mere rereading of materials be considered studying. Rather, the recall of ideas read can be greatly enhanced by systematically following several steps in study-type reading: (a) skimming to get the general ideas presented and to set purposes for reading, these are usually questions to be answered from the reading, which may be written down; (b) careful reading, to find answers to questions; (c) self-questioning about the content, using the questions and answers as a guide; and (d) recall of the questions and answers at intervals until a test is given, since humans forget much of what they learn very quickly. Variations of this technique can be taught to advanced students with profit. It is used especially for textbook materials in which the organizational pattern and typographical design greatly aid the skimming and question-posing.

A reader must learn to use many rates of reading if he is to be efficient. There are times—while reading a legal document or a new mathematical formula—when careful reading, with full attention to each word or component is necessary. A light novel may be read quickly, a newspaper can be skimmed, and a telephone book must be scanned. The reader makes unconscious decisions before and during reading about the most efficient rate to use. The use of skimming for all kinds of reading purposes, which is implicit in some speed-reading advertising, is not defensible. A far more satisfactory approach to the tasks of reading is adjusting the rate of reading to the purpose at hand. In operating an automobile, there are times when moving slowly is necessary. On the other hand, a broad open highway calls for a faster rate.

MATURITY IN READING

Modern preoccupation with speed and quantity tends to minimize quality of reading in favour of quantity. To provide a balance which restores the importance of quality in our reading, Gray and Rogers [4] proposed the concept of maturity in reading. They suggested that the mature reader exhibited these characteristics:

Genuine enthusiasm for reading.

Tendency to read (a) a wide variety of materials that contribute pleasure, widen horizons, and stimulate creative thinking; (b) serious materials which promote a growing understanding of one's self, of others, and of problems of a social, moral and ethical nature; and (c) intensively in a particular field or materials relating to a central core or radix.

Ability to translate words into meanings, to secure a clear grasp and understanding of the ideas presented, and to sense clearly the mood and feelings intended.

Capacity for and habit of making use of all that one knows or can find out in interpreting or construing the meaning of the ideas read.

Ability to perceive strengths and weaknesses in what is read, to detect bias and propaganda, and to think critically concerning the validity and values of the ideas presented and the adequacy and soundness of the author's presentation, views and conclusions. This involves an emotional apprehension, either favourable or unfavourable, as well as a penetrating intellectual grasp of what is read.

Tendency to fuse the new ideas acquired through reading with previous experience, thus acquiring new or clearer understandings, broadened interests, rational attitudes, improved patterns of thinking and behaving, and richer and more stable personalities.

Capacity to adjust one's reading pace to the needs of the occasion and to the demands of adequate interpretation.

Gray and Rogers suggested that these characteristics must be interpreted in terms of the reader's general maturity. If the reader has outgrown childish egocentricity and has developed an interest in the world outside himself, his selection of reading materials will be influenced by that fact and the social values or standards he has acquired will influence his interpretation of materials. In addition, they call attention to the desire of a mature reader to read extensively in many areas and intensively in subjects of specialization. The study of maturity in reading has only begun.

WHY ONE READS

Gray and Rogers have presented a carefully compiled list of purposes for reading which suggests that the habit of using reading is based upon real human needs. Variations in motivation for reading may occur in various cultures throughout the world, but this list of purposes provides a useful foundation:

As a ritual, or from force of habit.

From a sense of duty.

Merely to fill in or kill time.

To know and understand current happenings.

For immediate personal satisfaction or value.

To meet practical demands of daily living.

To further avocational interests.

To carry on and promote professional or vocational interests.

To meet personal-social demands.

To meet socio-civic needs and demands (good citizenship).

For self-development or improvement, including extension of
    cultural background.

To satisfy strictly intellectual demands.

To satisfy spiritual needs.

TIME SPENT IN READING

Many excuses are made by lapsed readers for not reading. Radio and television have been blamed, as have 'poor eyes', and 'too much work'. One never knows the truth in all cases, and we can always find exceptions—people with poor eyes who enjoy radio and television and do a lot of work and also read a great deal.

The background

Of the several case-studies of mature readers included in the Gray and Rogers study, the individual who was most nearly mature in all areas (Case Y-3), was a professional woman, whose activity in civic affairs contributed to her breadth and depth of interest, as well as her purposes for reading. Her awareness of these purposes was outstanding, as was the intellectual challenge of the material read, the richness of ideas involved and the varying difficulty of what she read. While some reading was at a level of great interest and penetration, some of it was at a superficial level, merely to satisfy a passing interest or whim. This was especially striking, however, for her schedule allowed very little time to spend in reading. She did not use the frequently heard excuse that there was not enough time for reading!

Much later, Kamarás [5] reported, in a quite different context, a similar finding. In spite of having less leisure time, Hungarian workers who were continuing their education were found to be reading greater quantities of material and also reading more often than those who were not continuing their schooling.

REFERENCES

1. BOND, Guy L.; DYKSTRA, Robert. The Comparative Program in First-Grade Reading Instruction. *Reading Research Quarterly*, Vol. II, No. 4, summer, 1967, p. 5–142.
2. SINGER, Harry; RUDDELL, Robert. *Theoretical Models and Processes of Reading*. Newark, Del., International Reading Association, 1976.
3. GRAY, William S. *The Teaching of Reading and Writing*. Paris, Unesco, 1956. 281 p.
4. GRAY, William S.; ROGERS, Bernice. *Maturity in Reading*. Chicago, Ill., University of Chicago Press, 1956. 273 p.
5. KAMARÁS, István. *The Workers and Reading*. Summary in English of *A Munkasok es az Olvasas*. Budapest, Netnüvelesi Propaganda Iroda, 1969.

Who influences reading?

An examination of the purposes for which people read suggests that there can be many reasons for engaging in the reading act. Some are clearly individual and personal, while others are societal, with many degrees of interrelationship between these two extremes of influences. The lover's appreciation of a certain poem may stem from the motivation provided by one individual and by his romantic feelings. How different is the vague, indirect encouragement to better oneself which stems from general societal pressures and general dissatisfaction with one's present station in life.

Why do some people read and others avoid books and reading? In a Unesco-sponsored symposium on reading motivation, a number of reasons for reading were discussed [1], and it was clear that the interplay of internal and external factors, rather than one single overriding element, was the key to understanding an individual's reading motivation. No man is an island and the customs and social and economic pressures which, for good or ill, impinge upon his life touch also upon his reading. This appears to be true of both the most mature reader and the least accomplished. The remainder of this chapter will consider some of the specific areas of influence upon our reading. We must recognize that they are not discrete, but often overlap greatly.

FAMILY INFLUENCES

'The family constitutes the first world of the child; ... by continuous, intimate, numerous, and varied associations it becomes a major source of education and behavior determination' [2].

All of us know of individuals who rose far above the station of their families, became rich and famous, and were the best, or only, educated members of their family. Perhaps they are interesting to us because they are unusual. The norm is that a person, shaped by the all-pervasive family, does not depart far from the family image.

Hence, a child who grows up surrounded by books and reading is likely to become a reader. There is, however, no guarantee that this will occur. Other factors are operative, each of which may encourage or discourage the reading habit.

It is generally accepted, however, that the models of reading found within a family, the reading materials which are easily available to the family, and the family attitudes towards learning what is in the world around us may form the foundation of the habit of reading.

THE WORLD OF THE READER

In Vienna, one seems surrounded by music. Almost everyone, it appears, plays a violin, sings, or frequents the concert halls and the famous opera house. Composers' birthplaces abound. If a visitor senses this musical atmosphere, what must be the effect on a Viennese, who has lived in the musical ambience of his city all his life? It is fair to say that the average Viennese child, growing up in this musical city, is more likely to understand, appreciate, and even to play music than a child from a place, which is musically less rich.

It is also probable that an individual growing up in an intellectually challenging world where there are many opportunities to find answers to questions, to expand intellectual horizons, and to interact with persons of similar interests, will be likely to be an avid reader.

Reading is usually considered a solitary activity. The personal nature of the act, with its interaction between the ideas of a writer and the brain of the reader, make this true. But there is also a pervading need to use the ideas gained from reading with other people. If exchange of the ideas read is not rewarded within the social structure in which the reader lives, it is inevitable that he will turn to solitary use and enjoyment of what he reads, and the enriching aspects of discussion, conflict and interaction are lost to him.

A study by Waples, Berelson and Bradshaw [3] hypothesized five basic reading effects. This list is useful to us because it presents various motivations of readers in broad personal and social terms.

The instrumental effect (e.g. fuller knowledge of a practical problem and greater competence to deal with it).

The prestige effect (e.g. relief of inferiority feeling by reading what increases self-approval).

The reinforcement effect (e.g. reinforcement of an attitude or conversion to another attitude toward controversial issues).

The aesthetic effect (e.g. obtaining aesthetic experience from specimens of literary art).

The respite effect (e.g. finding relief from tensions by reading whatever offers pleasant distraction).

Those of us in the book world must avoid falling into the trap, called by Ennis [4] 'the domination of the tool'. He said,

Give a young child a hammer, and he thinks the world is for hammering; give him a saw, and he thinks the world is for sawing. Reading can be some things, but it will not set the world right. The ordinary good sense and modesty that exist most of the time with respect to the power of books and reading often give way to strident overstatement and overselling in a market where everybody else is similarly touting his wares.

Reading is not the only avenue to learning about our world. To have this truth brought home, one needs only to experience a walk in the forest with a non-reader who knows all the plants and animals of the wild.

A basic determiner of the reading pattern seems to be social role or class when we consider social role as a constellation of intellectual, emotional and social characteristics. The reader brings his own world to the page. It enriches his reading, and when it is meagre, impoverishes his capacity for interpreting what he reads.

SCHOOLING

That education has an influence on continued learning has never been doubted by most people. Most of the evidence has been what social scientists would term soft evidence, however. There has been precious little hard test evidence, especially when the problem is considered across international lines. Recently, however, sociologists have been exhaustively comparing the available data in the United States, and Hyman *et al.* summarized existing firm evidence of the enduring effects of education [5]. The findings were that higher proportions of individuals with more formal schooling, compared to those with less schooling, regularly use the print media: newspapers, magazines and books. There is impressive evidence that education is positively related to newspaper reading, and the effects of education on subsequent adult reading is even more dramatic. The impact does not deteriorate with age.

The probability that an individual will read books is also a function of the amount of education. Hyman indicates [5, p. 86],

An average of 7 to 10 per cent of the elementary school educated in any age cohort were reading a book at the time of any of three independent surveys. In contrast, from 46 to 60 percent of the college graduates (on average) were currently reading a book. An average of 22 to 32 percent of the elementary school educated had read a book during the year preceding each of two surveys, while an average of 72 to 94 percent of the college graduates had done so.

This is a careful study which leaves little to chance. The greatest impediments to international comparisons were disruptive conditions such as war or natural catastrophes, which affected the adults or the educational systems being compared over a period of years, and the lack of educational attainment data. Recognizing that comparisons were perilous—asking the age of a respondent, for instance, is a recent innovation—a parallel analysis of Canadian data was made. The effects of Canadian education are 'also positive, substantial and enduring, and not unlike those found for the U.S.' [5, p. 121]. Perhaps, when the hard data are all in, the same conclusion can be drawn for other nations.

That education has an influence on reading cannot be denied; Gray and Rogers suggested that education 'is not seen as bearing a direct, simple, causal relationship to the reading pattern but rather as a clue to the social role, which is more nearly a determiner of the reading pattern' [5, p. 46]. Within the educated population, there are those who can, but do not read. Perhaps they could be called 'book-leavers'. Some have been conditioned in school to avoid reading. This conditioning has not been deliberate on the part of teachers or school authority, but it can have taken place subtly, through peer influence, through lack of appropriate materials in the school library, and not primarily through teacher activity. Whatever the responsibility of the teacher, for reading-leavers, it is clear that steps to combat this form of illiteracy should also be the school's responsibility.

INFLUENCE OF MEDIA

It is significant that in Hyman's consideration of the lasting effects of education he indicated that communications exposure is one prerequisite to informed social opinion. The mass media include newspapers, magazines and books as well as radio, television and the cinema. All are related and, using different means, lead towards the same end. Each has its own strengths—and weaknesses. The appeal of television, the portability of radio, and the social aspects of the cinema can influence reading; indeed they interact with it at many levels.

To brand the non-print media as 'the enemy' is shortsighted and inaccurate. One need only examine the sales figures of a novel which has just been serialized on television to observe an instance of the motivating nature of the interaction of the media.

The background

LIBRARIES

Jorge Luis Borges said, 'I was lucky to have been educated not only in schools—that was secondary—but in my father's library. . . . When I remember my childhood, I think less of the neighbourhood than of my father's library, and I think of those books that revealed the world to me' [6]. Most of us are not fortunate enough to have a private family library to browse through, to become educated in without being disturbed. Some of us—those of us who are favoured—have a school or public library at our disposal, if we will use it. At an early age, a school library can be a powerful influence to encourage reading, if books which appeal to children are made available. In addition, the ambience of a library is a factor. A child—or an adult, for that matter—who is repelled by the forbidding nature of a library will not stay long enough to taste its riches. Most librarians are dedicated to attracting the young, and to creating an inviting tone, especially in the children's department. Fortunately, attractive books for children are becoming available in increasing numbers, and in more languages than in the past.

One service of libraries which is often overlooked is the support which these institutions provide for *belles-lettres*. Since the expected sale of most fiction, poetry and essays is usually quite small, guaranteed sale to libraries makes it economically feasible for publishers to issue the works of new writers with lower risk. Hence, authors owe a debt of gratitude to libraries, and the public sees works which it would not have available except in manuscript form if libraries did not purchase them.

Another function of libraries is an outgrowth of the book and print explosion. It is impossible for any one person to remember all of the books available in even a small library. Therefore, the bibliographic function of librarians has become extremely important. Herman Liebaers, speaking for an international organization of librarians, has described it in this way,

The unique share of libraries in book promotion is the improvement of the accessibility to books through an adequate bibliographic coverage. Quick, accurate, and exhaustive information on books is the librarian's main objective. This is not as easy to achieve as to write it down in a simple phrase. To avoid any confusion I would like to add immediately that quite a number of trade catalogues, or even national bibliographies, are published commercially, but for our convenience I would consider these important contributions to book promotion as library work even when carried on outside libraries. And when one looks at this major problem of bibliographic control from a point of view which is not that of a few highly advanced countries, it becomes evident that only librarians can carry this burden. It is a burden and they should carry it. It is much more glamorous to write, to publish and to sell 'Jonathan Livingston Seagull' than to apply to it an internationally accepted standard bibliographic description. [7]

A system of 'Universal Bibliographic Control' has been devised, and there has also been launched an ambitious programme of co-ordination of national information systems through the auspices of Unesco. So that libraries will not wither on the vine through lack of funds, recommendations for legislative support of national systems have also been issued [8]. These should enhance the already important role of libraries in the provision and location of reading materials and the promotion of the reading habit.

BOOK-TRADE INFLUENCES

Publishers and booksellers have more than a direct financial interest in the encouragement of the reading habit. In making a book available, a publisher has contributed a high degree of creativity as well as a high degree of risk to the venture. The number of copies printed can rarely be matched with the demand. Too often, the publisher prints more copies than he can sell. One needs only to have responsibility for a pamphlet or small volume to appreciate the complexity of the tasks involved in the publication of a book. In addition to the literary selection which must be made, there are problems of design, editing/copy-preparation, typesetting, proof-reading, paper procurement, printing, binding, distribution and advertising. Each of these is critical and each has an influence on the prospective reader, albeit some influences are exerted at the subconscious level. Consider, for instance, the fact that each character of print presents a potential error by the typesetter and proof-reader; each page may be unsatisfactory if insufficient ink is used; and a group of sixteen or sixty-four pages which is misbound can cause confusion which makes the entire book useless to the reader. Even the smell of the ink, the paper or the glue used in binding has been known to discourage a reader from returning to a book.

Booksellers also provide service, help and advice, as well as books. Their service often involves locating the publisher, ordering, receiving, notifying the purchaser that a book is available and billing, as well as paying the publisher or distributor's invoice.

Service is not included in some outlets where books are stocked, especially for mass market sale, and the book purchaser is the loser. It is interesting to speculate on the number of book buyers who have not developed the habit of reading because they have not had the advantage of consulting an experienced bookseller for help and advice.

GOVERNMENT INFLUENCE

The idiosyncracies of governments are known to influence many things. The book world is not omitted, nor is the reader, even in the most *laissez-faire* government. As in most things, relations are healthiest when a balance is struck between intervention and neglect. The pervasive influence of government is clear in a paper-starved country in which indigenous publishing is encouraged, but no effort is made to relieve customs restrictions or double taxation of paper. There are many ways in which a government, or an individual government official, can help to promote reading and the book habit in his country.

The necessity of government support for an educational system and adequate training of teachers are universally recognized; however, the provision of school libraries must also be included as part of this support.

An indispensable tool of lifelong education is the public

library which is usually financed by public funds. Libraries accessible to prospective readers, with their shelves stocked and adequate staff to perform the function of locating as well as servicing materials, are another area where government action is essential.

Some countries provide special training facilities to encourage a skilled labour supply, and exempt books from customs duties and establish low postage rates for books, newspapers and periodicals as a measure of their support for the advantages which derive from a reading population.

The media have been shown to play an important supporting role in the promotion of the reading habit. Governments often support the media, and some encourage quality broadcasts, and discussions which may lead to reading through special grants or endowments.

Almost any activity which raises the intellectual sights of a people can be construed as promoting the reading habit. A government which is concerned about the future of a nation cannot help but be supportive of such activities.

REFERENCES

1. SULLIVAN, George. *A Reason to Read: A Report on an International Symposium on the Promotion of the Reading Habit*, p. 37–9. New York, N.Y., Academy for Educational Development, 1976.
2. HAYES, Waland J. The Family and Education. *Encyclopedia of Educational Research*, p. 433–5. Rev. ed. New York, N.Y., Macmillan Co., 1950.
3. WAPLES, Douglas; BERELSON, Bernard; BRADSHAW, Franklyn. *What Reading Does to People*. Chicago, Ill., University of Chicago Press, 1940.
4. ENNIS, Philip H. Reading, Revolution, and Human Need. *Reading and Revolution*, p. 56–63. Newark, Del., International Reading Association, 1970. (IRA Perspectives in Reading No. 13.)
5. HYMAN, Herbert H.; WRIGHT, Charles R.; REED, John Shelton. *The Enduring Effects of Education*. Chicago, Ill., University of Chicago Press, 1975.
6. BORGES, Jorge Luis. Libraries, Books and Reading. *Reading for All*, p. 4. Selected papers from the World Congress on Reading,

Buenos Aires, Argentine, 1972. Newark, Del., International Reading Association, 1973.
7. LIEBAERS, Herman. Book Promotion through Libraries. *Essays and Studies in Librarianship*, p. 49. Jerusalem, Magnes Press, 1975.
8. *Establishing a Legislative Framework for the Implementation of National Information Systems*. Paris, Unesco, 1977.

Changing reading habits

It would be agreeable if we had a magic wand, which when touched to the brow of a lapsed reader, would instantly transform him into an avid reader. What a market such magic would create!

The morning-after realization that no such magic wand will ever exist is inevitable, as is the grudging wish that we knew more about the process by which we work slowly towards the end of helping some lapsed readers overcome their apathy and make use of the riches which are available to them in books and reading. Change of any kind, however, is not easy to accomplish, and resistance to change often follows any effort to break away from old ways.

SUPPORTIVE INFLUENCES

If an individual who avoids reading is to alter his reading habits, support from many sources is necessary.

The value system of the culture in which he lives must reward a person for reading. So, also, must his respected peers. The economic system should reinforce the value of his reading. The educational system probably already does so, and the family may also praise his reading, although this cannot be guaranteed. Not all of these aspects of a culture will reward a reader simultaneously, and some may never provide support for his reading. In most cases, the encouragement which comes from these sources is vague and indirect; their influence nevertheless is strong and pervasive.

None of them is adequate if there is no means of providing books, magazines, or newspapers to the lapsed reader. If there exists no library, no bookseller, no potential for obtaining books by mail, or no friend with books to lend, the reader is likely to remain lapsed. There are stories of voyagers who carried precious books into the far corners of the world. Their motivation is usually clear, and their need for encouragement or support was slight.

In England, the self-motivated reader of the past was a product of his age—the early nineteenth century. The self-taught poet was romanticized, sought after, and publicized, and 'stirred literary ambitions in many humble breasts' [1, p. 241].

When books were scarce in England, they were extraordinarily precious to those who owned them. Altick quotes the reactions of William Cobbett, a 14-year-old son of a farmer-innkeeper, who 'saw in a Richmond bookseller's window a copy of *A Tale of a Tub*. It cost him 3 pence, his entire capital, and in the shade of a haystack in a corner of Kew Gardens he began to read. "The book", he recalled, "was so different from anything that I ever read before; it was something so *new* to my mind, that, though I could not at all understand some of it, it delighted me beyond description; and it produced in me a sort of birth of intellect" ' [1, p. 39].

It was very difficult to obtain books in that era. Altick's useful historical source quotes Lackington to the effect that

the barriers in the way of liberal indulgence in the taste for reading were formidable. Not merely were books themselves scarce except as the circulating library supplied them; shops in which to browse and people to give advice both were hard for the common reader to find. Lackington and a friend, journeymen cobblers in the late sixties, must have had counterparts enough among the literate young men of their class: they wanted to read books, 'but', wrote Lackington long afterward, 'so ignorant were we on the subject, that neither of us knew what books were fit for our perusal, nor what to enquire for, as we had scarce ever heard or seen any *title pages*, . . . [Hence] we were ashamed to go into the booksellers' shops; and . . . there are thousands now in England in the very same situation; many, very many have come into my shop who have discovered an enquiring mind, but were totally at a loss what to ask for, and who had no friend to direct them' [1, p. 40–1].

These tales are a century old, but in many ways they are new; a fellow-worker may still stimulate a reader, and an attentive, helpful bookseller (or teacher, or librarian) is often the bridge which a hesitant reader requires.

VARYING RATES OF CHANGE

Change in reading attitudes and habits is an individual matter; each reader's motivations are his own. But he is a part of a group and functions as a social being. Scientific observers have studied the adoption of new practices by groups of people and it is useful to see what they have found.

Even when the circumstances are ideal for change, not everyone changes at the same rate. Indeed, some do not change at all. This is an important fact to remember when designing a campaign to encourage people to do something differently.

One of the clearest descriptions of the way people vary as far as rates of change are concerned was used in a study of farmers' willingness to adopt new practices in agriculture [2]. The farmers surveyed were classified in five categories:

Innovators—the first to introduce new ideas or practices. They have the reputation in the community for doing so (3 per cent).

Early adopters—actively seek new ideas, and are quick to try them (13 per cent).

Early majority—generally receptive to new ideas, but do not actively seek them (34 per cent).

Late majority—less receptive to new ideas (34 per cent).

Late adopters—security-oriented, inclined to adhere to the tried and tested practices (16 per cent).

It can be seen that farmers are not the only group which can be subdivided into groups according to their willingness to adopt new ideas and practices. Fashion in dress, willingness to use new technology or tools, even the adoption of new religious practices demonstrate differences in attitudes towards new or different ideas. It can be hypothesized that some people are more prone to change their reading habits than others. Agencies responsible for improving the practices of farmers are quick to identify an 'early adopter' and to offer assistance to him, for he is a fertile means of spreading ideas to others.

So, too, it would be profitable if we could identify those lapsed readers who are most likely to change their habits. Unfortunately, we do not have the means to do so. Instead, another avenue has been taken by the book world—to provide resources and materials to encourage reading at the earliest ages. The steady growth of the children's book field in many countries of the world reflects this approach.

Youth is not an overriding factor in developing the reading habit. Thomas Holcroft, the English playwright and novelist, saw almost no books for six or seven years after leaving school and kept his reading skill alive by reading the ballads pasted on the walls of cottages and ale houses. When, much later, he became a shoemaker, one of his shopmates divided his leisure time between cock-fighting and reading! Reading was dominant, however, and after Holcroft had borrowed *Gulliver' Travels* and the *Spectator*, he was on the road to becoming a reader. In modern times, studies of the aged indicate that if they did not read in their middle age, they will not read when old age provides them with additional leisure time.

DIFFUSION OF CHANGE

A concept for describing the diffusion of adoption patterns may be useful in discussing the development of the reading habit. People appear to go through a series of distinguishable stages, according to Lionberger [3]. While these stages were first described in a rural setting, with farmers adopting changes in their methods, it is quite possible that they have application in many other areas. The stages, as described by Lionberger [3, p. 3-4], are:

Awareness—the first knowledge about a new idea, product or practice.

Interest—the active seeking of extensive and detailed information about the idea, to determine its possible usefulness and applicability.

Evaluation—weighing and sifting the acquired information and evidence in the light of the existing conditions into which the practice would have to fit.

Trial—the tentative trying out of the practice or idea, accompanied by acquisition of information on how to do it.

Adoption—the full-scale integration of the practice into the ongoing operation.

Application of these stages to the development of the habit of reading requires some amplification. While awareness that reading is useful in many activities, including problem-solving, can be thought to be a natural outgrowth of schooling, it may not be. Some individuals consider reading as an occupation irretrievably associated with schools, teachers and libraries. Activities of his peers can create an interest in reading about a specific subject, or a specific book or magazine. This may lead to conscious or, more likely, unconscious evaluation of the information of the profitableness of the reading activity which could lead to additional trial readings of other books and materials. Adoption requires a number of successful trials. Another way to look at these stages is to view them in the light of information-gathering.

The awareness that a source of information exists in a book may come from the media or from a friend. The prospective reader's interest can be aroused by specific needs which he has, by other information which he has previously encountered, by the accessibility of a book—in a store, through a friend, or, if he should be in one, a library or bookstore. The publisher may have used direct mail or other advertising to call attention to a specific book. This point of contact is of great importance, and is a fragile thing upon which the development of the reading habit may stand or fall. If the book is read, evaluation is accomplished, again consciously or unconsciously, by consideration of the appropriateness of the content to the needs of the reader, through discussion with peers, or by the opinions of outsiders. For continued trial and adoption, support from valued friends, as well as professional members of the book world—booksellers, librarians and publishers—is usually necessary. Each individual is different, and different influences operate. Therefore, a structure of stages which occur may be a useful tool in studying the development of the reading habit on the part of the public.

A reader rarely says, 'I am reading this book because . . .'. Reasons are not verbalized. Reading is a tool which is particularly useful for a given purpose, and it is used—just as a hammer might be used to hit a nail or a screwdriver to tighten a screw.

So, too, changes in reading habits are rarely talked about. They occur because both internal and external forces have influenced the reader, and reading materials were available to satisfy a need.

THE 'BOOKAHOLIC'

The 'bookaholic', whose story was told so amusingly by a journalist, Tom Zito [4], and reprinted in several newspapers including *The Guardian Weekly*, 24 July 1977, is the least likely to know why he needs to read books. Tongue in cheek, Zito writes,

Life without plenty of books lying around the house is like a day without orange juice for the bookaholic. Go a week without an acquisition and the hands start to shake. We're not talking of old books here. None of that snobby first-edition, out-of-print stuff. Just your basic on-the-shelf material that's waiting to be taken home. Bookaholism knows no bounds and blurs all borders. . . .

'The disease takes on new forms every year', says a young executive. 'I went through a particular period of stress once, and I developed a craving for big art books: *The Arts of China*, *The Horizon History of the British Empire*, *The Holy Land*. A college girl friend once accused me of taking more interest in my books than in her, which was right, and it planted a seed of doubt in my mind. I did not wed her.'

Most habitual readers are not nearly so extreme. Reading is, for them, not a conscious activity, and changes in their reading habits are also usually not conscious.

References

1. ALTICK, Richard D. *The English Common Reader*. Chicago, Ill., University of Chicago Press, 1957. 430 p.
2. ROGERS, E. M.; BEAL, G. M. *Reference Group Influence in the Adoption of Agricultural Technology*. Ames, Iowa, Iowa State University Press, 1958.
3. LIONBERGER, Herbert F. *Adoption of New Ideas and Practises*. Ames, Iowa, The Iowa State University Press, 1960.
4. ZITO, Tom. Bookaholics: The Big Escape. *The Guardian Weekly*, 24 July 1977. 18 p.

Part II

PROMOTING READING

Developing reading habits

Although many different kinds of book-promotion activities have been conducted, relatively few could be described as fully developed campaigns, utilizing many avenues of influence in a carefully planned and co-ordinated programme with built-in measures of success. Instead, most efforts have centred around specific, pin-pointed activities to increase the use of books and reading on the part of individuals and groups. This chapter will describe some of the most frequently employed devices, focusing on those that are innovative examples of their kind.

BOOK FAIRS AND BOOK WEEKS

Book fairs, book weeks, book festivals, etc., are to be found in many countries throughout the world. They may be organized on an international basis or at national or local levels. The examples that follow illustrate three ways by which such manifestations may be organized: through the efforts of volunteer groups; by professional book associations; and with the expertise of outside enterprises hired for the purpose.

'For the Love of Books'—Canada

The enthusiasm of the organizer of one successful experiment in organizing a book fair was reflected in the Canadian Book Publishers' newsletter, *Communiqué*. The report stands by itself.

Beginning from a standing start with no similar experience as a model, financed on a shoestring, and organized by a committee of volunteers, 'For the Love of Books' wound up its ten days having achieved a remarkable level of success. The 29 official exhibitors present represented over 150 Canadian book publishers. Estimated public attendance, in spite of bad weather on the two weekends, was 15,000, 50% higher than predicted. Receipts from book sales totalled almost $7,000, close to three times the most pessimistic projection and as much as 40% above more optimistic advance estimates.

Reports from a variety of outside sources indicate that the venture was a success in its primary objective of attracting favourable attention to Canadian books. For example, during the five weekdays, 3,500 school children visited the fair with their teachers for specially arranged tours. Harbourfront officials estimate that at least another 6,000 would have attended if it had been possible to accommodate them. Representatives of both the federal and provincial governments who attended were equally enthusiastic in their reactions and have encouraged the venture. Perhaps most important, although impossible to quantify, was public reaction. It was clear to all who were in attendance regularly, that many of the fair's visitors were not those who regularly patronize bookstores or normally take an interest in books. It was also evident that many people were astonished by the number and diversity of Canadian titles on display. Above all, the attention given by the media and the many comments of visitors demonstrated that the public responded extremely favourably.

To be fair, of course, the positive must be balanced by the acknowledgment of some disappointments. Organizational strains (hopefully less evident on the outside than on the inside) brought their share of headaches. Some publishers' displays probably did not rise to an adequate standard for a public presentation and very few publishers availed themselves in any way at all of the potential for publicity offered by the fair.

'For the Love of Books' began with a request for a book display from Harbourfront, a federally sponsored recreational and cultural facility in central Toronto. The initial approach was made to the Canadian Book Design Committee, Inc., which was subsequently joined by a variety of organizations and associations in the book publishing and related industries, including the Canadian Book Publishers' Council, the Association of Canadian Publishers and the Canadian Booksellers Association. The organizing committee consisted of representatives of these groups.

In organizing 'For the Love of Books', the committee had in mind several objectives, the primary one being to create an event that would help to focus attention on publishing, writers and books at the beginning of the fall season. Although such an event is new to Toronto, the basic concept is by no means unique. . . . 'For the Love of Books' was an experiment to see if what had proved successful elsewhere could be added to the Toronto scene and, more generally, to the Canadian book scene.

What, then, about the future? Should 'For the Love of Books' be repeated? The decision will, of course, depend upon the response of the publishers and the sponsoring organizations, but the success of this year's fair has demonstrated convincingly that the concept can be developed. Moreover, the Secretary of State's plans as described by him at the opening of 'For the Love of Books', for an annual book fair occurring on a rotating basis in various Canadian cities across the country is obviously not unrelated to the potential development of an annual book fair in Toronto or any other city. If it can be done elsewhere, why not in Canadian cities? If an initial experiment with limited resources can succeed, why cannot something based on that experience and with a significantly improved programme be even more successful? [1]

'Festival of Books'—Singapore

The compact Republic of Singapore, with four official languages, has, through the National Book Development Council of Singapore and the Singapore Book Publishers Association, sponsored a 'Festival of Books' designed for the general public, and including a book fair held in one of the large hotels. Expenses of the ten-day celebration were provided by the rental paid by thirty-three exhibitors in eighty-one stalls who took part in the book fair. Singapore publishers of materials in English, Chinese, Malay and Tamil, as well as overseas publishers participated.

Additional funds were obtained from advertisements in an attractive publication, the Festival of Books issue of the *Singapore Book World*, official organ of the council. This sixty-four-page publication was distributed free during the festival, and is in itself a testament to the varied and well-organized activities which are a part of the book development programme in Singapore.

Publisher involvement, both with the council and with the

festival/book fair was critical to their success. Publishers provided the winning book mark designed by students in a competition, and polyethylene bags with the festival and book fair design which were used in sales of books at the fair.

Programmes and posters were distributed to all universities, and the Ministry of Education, which is a member of the National Book Development Council, distributed copies to all 500 schools in the republic. Schoolchildren were also involved in the bookmark design contest, in Malay and Chinese poetry-writing competitions for secondary school students, as well as short play/story-telling and painting contests for elementary school students. All competitions except one were organized by the National Library. The Library Association of Singapore organized an essay contest on libraries in conjunction with the festival.

In addition to exhibiting at the book fair, booksellers displayed posters and distributed book marks as promotion for the festival. One bookseller also organized an autograph session by local authors during the fair.

Cinema advertising for the festival was provided free of charge by theatres, and paid advertisements were included in the local press, including English, Malay, and Chinese newspapers. Film shows, with no admission charge, were arranged by the National Library. Radio interviews with the council chairman as well as with several authors and other participants were arranged by Radio and Television Singapore, a branch of the Ministry of Culture.

Government involvement in the festival was primarily through agencies which are members of the National Book Development Council. These included the National Library, which is also the public library of Singapore, and the Ministry of Culture. This department organized the distribution of posters to schools, community centres, shopping centres, bus stops, and similar high-traffic areas.

Since the council has no paid staff, all work done for the festival was voluntary. The design used for the poster, an advertising brochure, the polyethylene shopping bag and the cover of the special issue of *Singapore Book World* was provided by one volunteer free of charge. Judges for the various competitions and for the National Book Awards were also unpaid volunteers. The only paid personnel were the publishers' staff members who were assigned to the Festival of Books as a part of their regular function.

The number of visitors to the eighth Singapore Book Fair, which culminated the activities of the 'Festival of Books', was estimated to be about 40,000 persons; cash sales at the fair were about $(S)125,000 in the ten-day period. These cold figures do not communicate the high degree of involvement with books and reading which resulted from the preliminary activities, contests, displays, advertising, and media publicity.

'*OZBOOKWEEK*'—*Australia*

An example of how a professional public relations firm can be used to promote a book-week celebration is exemplified in the 'OZBOOKWEEK' in Melbourne. Although 'OZBOOKWEEK' was held on 18–26 October 1975, formal activities started in May and carried through November of that year.

The main objective of the campaign was to reach the 65 per cent of the Australian public who are not regular book purchasers. The public relations firm reported that OZBOOK-WEEK was an unqualified success. Most of the information on the promotion derives from a report to the National Book Council from a public relations firm in Melbourne. The introduction to this report provides useful background information. It is somewhat telescoped here for space reasons:

On Monday, May 12, 1975, International Public Relations was appointed by the Australian Book Week Promotion Committee of the National Book Council 'to carry out all promotions connected with the Australian Book Week 1975'. The broad outlines of the brief were:
To sharpen awareness in the community of Australian books.
To increase the instance and frequency of buying and borrowing of Australian books.
To stimulate interest in Australian books.
To enhance the attitudes of the Australian public to Australian books.

Campaign Palace were appointed to produce all design and artwork for Australian Book Week. Both companies were to be directly responsible to the Australian Book Week Promotion Committee. This point is stressed early in the report, as several members of book trade organisations seem to have been under the impression that both organisations were responsible to the entire book trade.

As the project gathered momentum, I.P.R. became almost a full-time secretariat for Australian Book Week. The sheer volume of administrative detail put great difficulties in the way of our main purpose—to create promotional and publicity opportunities for Australian Book Week. I.P.R. consultants and staff spent a total of 1,180 hours on this assignment. In addition, the National Book Council paid for $126\frac{1}{2}$ hours of labor for distribution of material.

Initially, it was understood that Australian Book Week would be subsidized to $50,000 by the Literature Board of the Australia Council. The budget as first presented to the Literature Board by the Chairman of the National Book Council amounted to $56,500. The expenditure was finally limited to $45,000. In broad terms, the Committee felt that 60% of the Budget should be spent in reaching the 'unconverted' reader, 30% directed to the 'converted' reader, and 10% to professional fees.

In order to co-ordinate the physical aspects of the campaign, a well-known marketing consultant was appointed to handle themes and designs. It was recommended that a logo not be used as a symbol or trademark, largely because it is not possible to have a logo work properly in the short period surrounding Australian Book Week. They indicated that most of the recognized logo designs used in advertising and publicity have had hundreds of thousands of dollars spent on them before they became familiar.

One member of the Australian Book Week Promotion Committee observed:

It is important that the name of the promotional week be memorable, human and in the common language. It is felt that Australian Book Week fails in regard to this criteria. It is cold, bureaucratic and unimaginative. It does not have any creative spark—and this, in a field where creativity is all-important.

The selection of an alternative name is not an easy task. The prime prospect to whom we are addressing our promotional activities must be considered. In this regard, we are setting out to reach almost every age and socio economic group. Hence the name must be as broadly appealing as possible.

Eventually, the name 'OZBOOKWEEK' was decided upon, as a memorable, different and informal title for this book-week celebration. 'OZ' was derived from a shortened version of 'Australia' which appears to be accepted equally by the different groups of Australians, which were the target audience.

The promotional activities were tied to individual books by the use of an especially designed Australian book seal, which could be affixed to book covers, and so specify that this was an Australian book. The design was also used in advertising, in general publicity, and in conjunction with display material of various kinds.

In all, 8,000 posters, 100,000 bookmarks, 100,000 seals were provided, and advertising was programmed to be used in a retail context, and retailers were expected to utilize these point-of-sale aids as a part of their merchandising for Australian Book Week. In addition to providing materials to 300 large retail bookstores and 100 department or chain stores, they were also sent to 700 public libraries and 1,480 secondary school libraries. Although 11,000 yellow OZBOOKWEEK information sheets were distributed to booksellers and publishers for purposes of planning their merchandising campaigns, an additional 2,500 had to be printed subsequently to meet the demand. As another indication of the demand for materials, by the end of the book week the organizers had run completely out of seals, except for a few kept for archival purposes, and only 100 posters and 200 bookmarks were left.

Newspapers were encouraged to run either enlarged book features or special supplements on books, which would help spread the message of OZBOOKWEEK. Each country newspaper was sent a package of at least twenty book reviews and additional editorial matter relating to Australian writing and publishing. These were published in twenty-four large and small newspapers, and it was estimated from reliable statistics that over 4 million readers saw the OZBOOKWEEK message at the beginning of the week. Smaller retailers advertised in the special supplements developed from these materials. The supplements were not supported by enough advertising from publishers and large booksellers, according to the organizers.

Supporting activities included a display competition featuring 'Our Favourite Australian Books' to which publishers donated books valued at $3,335 as prizes. Bookshops, regional, municipal and school libraries were invited to enter the competition and sent posters, seals and bookmarks. So much interest was shown that the closing date for entries had to be extended for about a month. Prizes were awarded on the basis of photographs (which caused some delays) and an entry form which summarized the main features of the display and was supplemented by special reports of supporting activities.

In some places, special ceremonies inaugurating OZBOOK-WEEK attracted a wider audience for the display and aroused interest in Australian books. Some booksellers bought space in local newspapers and used other media to draw attention to the displays. Press clippings submitted by the entrants indicated that the displays produced extensive editorial and pictorial coverage. Book lists of Australian books in the display were distributed, and in some cases, books available for borrowing from the local library or for sale at bookshops were made available. Added strength was gained through the involvement of many persons not connected with the book trade in the display competition. Display staff, children, amateur photographers, all participated enthusiastically. A librarian in a small high school wrote of the results,

I doubt that any of the 3,000 inhabitants of our Shire were not made aware of OZBOOKWEEK. Most of the students have been wholeheartedly behind this activity and they worked together as a team. Perhaps this competition has been one of the best things to encourage such school spirit.

A costumed creature known as the Ozbookworm personified the celebration in many ways, and was seen by an estimated 24,000 persons. He presented the Lord Mayor of Melbourne with a special book (Liardet's *Water Colours of Old Melbourne*, issued by the University of Melbourne Press) at the opening ceremony. In Sydney, an Ozbookworm appeared for five days, for about three minutes each day in an excellent series of television appearances. Ozbookworm also appeared in department stores and city bookstores. A recommendation was made for a children's television series on the adventures of 'Ozbookworm in Literature Land'. The actors who portrayed the Ozbookworm reported that he created an instant audience with both young and old.

Many other opportunities to publicize OZBOOKWEEK were taken all over Australia. In each of the six large cities, where the great majority of the country's population lives, activities, such as radio and television interviews, special story-telling sessions, and dinners were held.

In conjunction with OZBOOKWEEK two awards were made to Australian authors for books published within a twelve-month period which have high literary merit. There were five outstanding books, according to the three judges, and so of the $5,000, $4,000 was divided equally among the five authors, and the $1,000 publishers prize was similarly distributed. In addition, five books received special commendation. The awards were announced at a gala dinner in a Sydney hotel, with appropriate remarks, in the presence of a number of important persons interested in books and reading. Dustjackets of all Australian books published during the year were displayed, and the award-winning books were highlighted.

A great deal of the publicity had been planned around the winner of the annual award, and the public relations firm had successfully negotiated for a major story on the awards. The result is a lesson in the difficulties of dealing with the press. The report says,

We were extremely concerned, therefore, to be faced with a five-winner award story. To quote a senior ABC journalist: 'One winner is a story—two winners indicates either discord among the judges, or superlative excellence, and could be a story. NO winners would be a tremendous story, but five winners is no story at all.'

There was some coverage of the award story, but it is obvious that it was disappointing to the organizers.

Adapters of the Ozbook scheme in other places will thank the public relations firm which co-ordinated the activities for the candid comments which were included in their report. It can be seen that the activities engaged in for OZBOOKWEEK were of a type quite acceptable for business and merchandising public relations campaigns. They were for the most part commercial rather than literary. As a result—and other factors must have been involved—the original assumption of the consultants that the entire book trade was wholeheartedly behind Australian Book Week was found to be not totally true. Some members of the trade gave courteous support, rather than whole-hearted backing.

The consultants recommended that in the future, members of the Book Trade Group be invited to take a larger part in the promotion. Although delegates from the major industry bodies were represented on the Promotion Committee, it became obvious that some delegates did not fully ensure that members of their organization were properly informed of planned activities. Many members of one group contacted the consultants directly, which indicated that they had a most garbled idea of the plans that had been made.

The need for active participation by all members of the book community was made obvious by another incident which militated against the success of OZBOOKWEEK. A massive campaign generated on behalf of two controversial Australian writers the previous week thwarted efforts to place authors with the media during OZBOOKWEEK. The early campaign regrettably included no mention of the coming book-week celebration.

The fact that most literary editors of newspapers did not co-operate with book-week activities was disappointing to the consultants. The feature and general editors as well as writers on subjects of interest to women wrote about OZBOOKWEEK, analysed it and contributed to the promotion of Australian books on their pages. The success of the original aim, to reach those who are not regular book purchasers, was pointed up by the fact that the strongest support for OZBOOKWEEK came from what is known as the 'people's' media. These radio and newspaper correspondents saw and appreciated the value of focusing the attention of the non-book buying public on books.

BOOK CLUBS

Book clubs and reading associations are another means of stimulating reading habits. A particularly successful example of this type of activity may be found in the Book-lovers' Association of the Union of Soviet Socialist Republics.

Although 4 million books are published every day in the Soviet Union, according to official figures, there is a demand for still more books. The Book-lovers' Association's priority aim is to help speed up the book distribution system. It does so by encouraging the use of private collections of members, by promoting contacts between publishers, book distribution centres, and libraries in order to improve the mutual exchange of literature and by establishing museums of literature and books [2].

Centres are located in fifteen federal republics and are responsible for establishing a network of book-lovers' clubs at various levels (regional, district, autonomous republic, national area and urban district) whose members meet either at a club near their place of work, or at one near their residence. These bodies appoint committees whose task is to co-operate with the Book-lovers' Association in fields ranging from literature and libraries, the activities of second-hand book dealers, literary critics and collectors of albums, postcards, and pamphlets to graphic art in books.

The association is directed by an Academician, and has as its most noteworthy function a Congress of Bibliophiles, which meets every five years. In the interim between sessions, the affairs of the association are conducted by a steering committee appointed by the congress. Similar associations, it is reported, are also being established in the federal republics. Well-known persons in the world of science and culture, writers and journalists are members of the regional bodies responsible for the organizations organizing these associations in the republics. At the last report, steering committees had been set up for the RSFSR, Ukrainian SSR, Uzbek SSR, Kazakh SSR and Georgian SSR.

The association's activities are varied. It organizes literary evenings for book-lovers, with the participation of writers, story-tellers and musicians. Here, the book-lover can meet the author of his favourite book, a publisher, or he can relax, listen to music or obtain a book he wants. New works are discussed at lectures on literature. The book distribution centres organize such events as book fairs or book-sale fortnights with the participation of writers, graphic artists, and others from the book world.

The association helped to organize the first exhibition of the private collections of book-lovers in the Republic of Estonia. An exhibition organized by the 'Soviet Russia' publishing house at Chelyabinsk was a popular success. At a National Book Exhibition in Moscow, to celebrate the thirtieth anniversary of victory in the Second World War, an exhibit was organized around the slogan, 'Fighting Book'. Similar exhibitions have been organized in the various republics, provinces, and regions of the Soviet Union.

In addition, the association publishes a book review, circulates information for book-lovers, and publishes special editions. It has workshops for the restoration of rare books and the production of equipment for use in private libraries.

In Israel, another approach has been used. After six years of experimentation and a lifetime of teaching and studying and teaching reading in Israel, Ilie Stanciu set up a method of encouraging reading through the use of reading clubs. These informal, but structured organizations are especially designed for adolescents and adults. They attempt to maintain a cultural background in a pleasant pressure-free atmosphere, provide members with varied information through many media, and try to develop sensitivity to reading while encouraging participants to expand their horizons through reading.

The reading clubs can be adopted to many age and cultural levels, to various physical sites such as schools, libraries, community centres, armed forces centres, and immigrants centres. A guide has been issued which is especially designed for underprivileged adolescents, male and female, who attend educational centres [3].

MASS MEDIA

The use of the mass media to promote books and reading is an avenue many countries have found worth exploring. For example, the Brazilian Government periodically sponsors radio and television broadcasts designed to develop an interest in reading. Spot announcements in commercial format are called 'Ler é Viver' (To Read is to Live). These announcements, which are broadcast throughout the day, include poems and passages from well-illustrated novels. Brazilian libraries report an increase in circulation as a result of these 'commercials'.

In Austria, the national radio and television has inaugurated a programme to encourage reading entitled *Lies Mit* (Read Along). It reaches about 2 million households, and offers prizes of books and book coupons for the completion of reading tasks. It is sponsored by the radio and television authority with the active co-operation of the Austrian book trade, including both publishers and booksellers.

In the United Republic of Tanzania, radio has been used to maintain the reading impetus generated by the government's mass literacy campaigns.

More than 6,000 free radio sets have been distributed for the use of listening groups developed from successful literacy programmes. The pattern of programmes which are designed to stimulate reading is as follows: usually a topic is discussed by a specialist and, toward the end of the programme, mention is made of publications which could be used to obtain more information about the subject. Page numbers and other specific directions are given.

Related discussion topics, in addition to the motivational programmes mentioned above, are: continuing education by using the library, book-borrowing rules, how to spend leisure time, how to use books for group discussion, how to use newspapers, the library and the teacher, the rural library service, and what should be read and what there is to be read.

After each topic has been discussed on the radio, a discussion question for the listening group is announced. An example of one of these questions is: 'What do we gain through reading books, newspapers or other reading materials?'

In an evaluation of the radio education motivation and functional series, it was found that 69 per cent of the respondents in a representative sample indicated that they read more books and newspapers as a result of the programme. It is important to note that these reading materials were obtained from many sources, including, of course, the rural libraries, but also from teachers and supervisors, from neighbours and friends, school libraries, co-operative societies and political party offices. In addition, some readers bought books as they were available.

NEW LITERATES

Special problems exist in developing countries that have embarked on massive literacy campaigns. All too often, it has been found that large proportions of newly literate adults lapse back into illiteracy for lack of sufficient reading material geared to their special needs and interests. Maintaining and improving reading skills, motivating adults who have never read before to adopt the reading habit, and providing the right books and periodicals in adequate quantities are among the challenges to be met through a combination of foresight and careful planning.

In Brazil, this is being accomplished through co-operation between an independent publishing trade and a strong government sponsored mass literacy effort called 'MOBRAL'.

The planners of this well-organized literacy programme recognized the need for an ongoing cultural programme to follow its programmes for Functional Literacy and Integrated Education [4]. The plans for 'Cultural MOBRAL', as this follow-up programme is called, recognized the need to expand the cultural universe of the Brazilian population in general and that of the 'Mobralites' in particular. The MOBRAL public, they indicated, is characterized by a low level of formal schooling, a limited cultural horizon and, in almost all cases, low purchasing power. The general scope of 'Cultural MOBRAL', it was suggested, should include an informal, flexible and dynamic contribution to the expansion of the cultural environment of the MOBRAL pupil and of the Brazilian population as a whole. It aims to develop the various potentialities of each individual, to stimulate sensitivity, and to endeavour to raise the professional qualifications of the people and to arouse their feelings of self-confidence.

In order to achieve these goals, which should necessarily be linked to the most varied forms of artistic and cultural activity, MOBRAL has signed agreements with cultural agencies such as Instituto Nacional do Libro (National Book Institute), Instituto Nacional do Cinema (National Cinema Institute), Meseu da Imagem e do Som (Audio-visual Museum) and Servico Nacional do Treatro (National Theater Agency). These agreements were designed to provide activities to fill leisure hours.

The operational system of the 'Cultural MOBRAL' programme was based, in its initial phase, on mobile units called 'Mobraltecas' (MOBRAL libraries) and fixed units called 'Cultural Posts'. In a second stage the Feiras Culturais (Culture Fairs) are expected to be introduced. These fairs are planned as travelling displays of the cultural activities of a given state or region, promoting an exchange among local cultures, and encouraging the process of national integration.

In view of the enormous size of Brazil and the wide network of MOBRAL posts, mobile units, the 'Mobraltecas', are proposed to support the various cultural activities scheduled. In accordance with the range of material to be built up through previously mentioned agreements, these mobile units would seem to represent the most adequate way to serve these sectors of the population heretofore deprived of information and having no means of access to artistic and cultural activities.

It is planned that the Mobraltecas will have a library, television receiver and video-tape equipment, sound equipment, film projectors and film-strips and slide projectors. With this equipment, it should be possible to show all forms of art and culture included in the collection of a Mobralteca.

The Mobraltecas were expected, in addition to this, to be equipped with film camera and regular photographic equipment, which would record habits, customs, types of work, landscapes, etc., in the various localities through which it passes.

In brief, the 'Cultural MOBRAL' programme was planned to set into motion a complete process which should culminate in permanent cultural activities throughout the entire country, while at the same time sparking the improvement of all forms of culture throughout Brazil.

In addition, a radio programme called *Integrated Education* is envisaged. This is, to a large extent, to bring motivation for reading and other cultural attainments, and was described as follows:

The programme will cover a period of 16 months, in four stages of 4 months, permitting pupils, in accordance with their individual characteristics and cultural attainments, to receive a certificate of course completion after due evaluation. The programme will call for maximum attention to the individual potentialities. With this in mind, the teaching staff will be specially trained in dealing with heterogeneous classes containing diversified groups.

MOBRAL has had broad-based backing from government and the publishing industry, has been carefully and systematically planned, and adjustments have been made as needed. The Mobralteca programme, it has been reported, is now engaged in preparing reading material for those people who have just finished the initial course for illiterates.

An entirely different programme is being carried out in the United Republic of Tanzania, a nation of 937,000 square kilometres and 15 million persons, where the great problem is providing for the expected 5 million persons who will in 1980 have become literate through functional literacy programmes. The lack of suitable materials, especially in rural areas where the majority of people live, and of the type which are specifically oriented towards development have been identified by the

Ministry of Education as needs which must be considered. Two additional problems were cited: (a) the lack of specific facilities and an integrated support mechanism for distribution; and (b) the need for new readers to move from 'mere reading' to habits of reading 'to learn and apply'.

According to the ministry, the national efforts in the eradication of illiteracy have taken into consideration the following needs:

That methods and approaches be established in order to check the relapse into illiteracy by the new literates.

That the knowledge and skills acquired by participants in the functional literacy programme be further strengthened.

That some persons, who having gone through the formal system of education, have relapsed into illiteracy partly because of lack of reading materials and facilities.

That since literacy and adult education as development factors are being manipulated or are operating within and upon a largely illiterate environment background, there is a need for the creation of a literacy and learning environment.

That since literacy and adult education are accepted factors in the national development strategy, there is the necessity to create facilities for the provision of lifelong functional education.

The Tanzanian programme includes setting up simple village libraries to provide reading material to adults who have attained literacy; a radio programme to encourage the development of reading habits; writers' workshops to encourage the development of suitable reading materials and editorial competence, and, for those who do not like to read books, the development of rural newspapers.

The first few libraries were formed in 1969 in the Lake Zones and the number has gradually increased with time so that at present all of the 2,000 wards in the republic have been provided with a rural library, each serving about 7,000 to 10,000 persons. There are altogether over 2,000 ward libraries. The ultimate goal is to have a library in each village.

The ward library is expected to be stocked with 500 book titles, two copies of each title. Most of the books are purchased from commercial publishers while the rest are produced by the Ministry of National Education as a result of the efforts made by the Writers' Workshops. All these books are distributed freely to the libraries. The books purchased from commercial publishers cost, on average, about U.S.$1 each.

Local authorities are being encouraged to erect standardized buildings for housing these libraries, but at present the libraries are located in a number of places including primary schools, dispensaries, local courts, co-operative societies, etc., and in private homes.

The library is manned by a trained part-time ward librarian who has been provided with a bicycle and a book-box or bag for circulating books to the outlying villages. The library usually opens for a few hours every afternoon to allow library users to borrow or read the books and newspapers. An experiment is currently taking place in the Lake Zone, by providing pressure lamps, so that libraries may be used in the evenings. The librarian is paid a small honorarium of about U.S.$4 per month.

In order to strengthen the functioning and utilization of the library, the librarian encourages the formation of a discussion group composed of library members. The purpose of the group is to have members discuss some of the material they have read and which could be of interest and practical relevance to their local situations and perhaps through discussion be able to arrive at decisions for solving the day-to-day problems.

In reality, library users are not only those persons who have gone through the literacy programme, although these are the majority, but also those who have gone through the formal system of education.

The studies carried out so far have indicated that library users would prefer to read fiction and books dealing with political, academic, Swahili language development, home economics and agricultural themes.

It should also be mentioned that the Swahili daily national newspaper *Uhuru* carries a special page for the new reading public.

The Ministry of National Education, in commenting on the United Republic of Tanzania's overall efforts, stated,

The introduction of these innovations into an environment where reading habits are virtually non-existent requires concerted motivational efforts and actions so that these innovations may succeed. These motivational efforts and actions may, for example, include elements such as educating the communities on the importance and relevance of the facilities which have been provided; encouraging the communities to erect library buildings on self-help basis; providing the librarian with a bicycle and book-box for circulating the books in outlying villages; organizing discussion groups; selling the newspaper at a token price; introducing suitable books for the new literates and rural adults; the creation of other institutions which could support the innovations [5].

REFERENCES

1. 'For the Love of Books'. *Communiqué*, Canadian Book Publishers' Newsletter, November/December 1977, p. 18–9.
2. USSR. *Book Promotion News* (Unesco), September 1975, p. 8. (Newsletter No. 7.)
3. STANCIU, Ilie. *Clubs for the Encouragement of Reading. Excerpts from a Guide*. Jerusalem, Henrietta Szold Institute for Research in the Behavioural Sciences, 1977.
4. *The Mobral System*. Rio de Janeiro, Fundaçao Movimento Brasilero Brasiliero Alfabetizaçao, 1973.
5. *Reading Habits Motivational Campaigns*. Mwanza, United Republic of Tanzania, National Literacy Centre, 1977.

Reading research

A vital element in the success of any campaign to promote books and reading is the availability of accurate and comprehensive data on reading habits, skills, motivation, etc.

Since Gutenberg's time, the German book world, for example, has paid great attention to studying the problems of the book culture. Gutenberg's momentous step forward of transforming the copyist's single book to the many volumes made possible by the modern printing press was a technical one. The modern German-language book world continues to be technically advanced, but this is superseded for every editor, publisher and bookseller by the availability of knowledge and information about the market for books, the character of readers and book purchasers and, in general, the kinds of information which can be used to make intelligent decisions about his work. In addition, the international book trade utilizes the Frankfurt Book Fair each October to foster its general and its individual interests. Translation rights, more important than ever, are traded and sold in ever-increasing quantities each autumn at that enormous book fair.

How does this influence motivation for reading? If one compares reading materials to any other merchandise which is for sale, it is the responsibility of the seller to provide goods which the buyer wishes to purchase. To a certain extent, the more the publisher knows about the market and its desires, the more likely it is that books will be sold. A bookseller, or any other retail outlet is successful in business to the extent that the public buys merchandise. Of course, buying books or any other reading material does not mean that they will be read, but it is a positive indicator.

What kind of information is collected to be made available for decision-makers in the German-language book world? The 'German reading culture' is periodically surveyed for the trade association, the Boersenverein des Deutschen Buchhandels. Comparisons are made every five years. The 1974 collection of studies was based on answers from a panel composed of about 1,000 individuals. Data were obtained to help answer the large question, 'How can the market for books be fostered?' Although the questions derive from marketing research, their responses have important sociological and social-psychological meaning. In his introduction, Schmidchen [1, p. 709] comments, 'The motivation to read books and to acquire them is, at least, related to all of these: the social structure, the quality of social role, the habit of using information, and the existence of a reading culture.'

Some of the topics upon which these carefully and thoroughly conducted studies gather and compared information were: reading and other leisure-time activities, reading books for entertainment, reading books for personal development, frequency of book reading, last time you read a book, frequency of reading 'novels', personal ownership of books, number of books in the household, persons, according to education, in the household, and books they own, amount spent on books, importance of books to you, importance of books in your cultural milieu, cognitive and affective values of books, attitudes towards children's reading, uses of books, how and where reading takes place, books as gifts, attitudes towards spending money for books, where books are purchased, sales items which 'do not belong' in a bookstore.

Not only are data collected for topics such as those mentioned above, but subtle and sophisticated statistical comparisons are made to show relationships and trends in these periodic studies.

In the developing countries as well, there is growing awareness of the importance of basic research to provide the insights necessary to formulating programmes specially geared to local needs and conditions. In Brazil, for example, an exploratory sociological study [2] of the influences which produce reading habits was conducted by the Latin American Centre for Research in the Social Sciences by a team which investigated the influence of the family on reading. Fifty families of varying socio-economic levels, varying sizes, and with children of different ages were carefully studied, and their reading of various kinds was analysed. Several factors emerged as having significant influence on the habit of reading. First was the existence of privacy in which reading could take place. Since reading is a relatively solitary activity which requires some degree of concentration, this finding was not a surprise. Second, the purchase of books by adults, indicating a value judgement, is also a reflection of socio-economic status. The third element which was believed to condition reading habits, as measured in the study, was the presence of at least one adult who lives with the family, or who visits the family regularly, who reads frequently.

Another study of broad sociological significance was conducted by Bosi and published in 1972 [3]. Dealing with the popular culture, and focusing especially on the reading of workers in São Paulo, it is quite possible that this study influenced the formation of the MOBRAL movement mentioned in the preceding chapter.

The reasons for lack of reading, the sources of reading materials (40 per cent of those purchased were obtained at the factory gate), and the kinds of materials read were studied. In addition, the topics of interest, and those sought out in newspapers, magazines and books were included.

A particularly important area for study and research is related to reading habits among children. An example is the recent study of the reading behaviour, reading performance, and reading interests of 10-year-old children in Austria [4]. A sampling of 2,398 children participated: 1,528 from rural areas and small towns, 379 from larger towns of 100,000, and 491 from the capital city of Vienna. The children and their teachers responded to carefully constructed questionnaires. For example, one question for children was, 'When do you read in your leisure time?' Possible answers were: (a) never; (b) daily; (c) now and then; (d) only on Sunday. Another question in the battery read, 'Do you remember the last time you had nothing to do?

What did you do? How long?' Finally, a list of free-time activities was drawn up, and each child was asked to choose the three which were most preferred. By asking the same question in different fashion, a valid picture of how reading fared in a child's leisure time preferences was obtained.

The teachers provided much information about each child in their questionnaire. Socio-economic level, parents' occupations, reading characteristics, and comparisons with the remainder of the class were among the data derived from teachers' responses. In addition, standardized reading tests were administered, as well as informal tests.

The analysis of the data was cautious, and the results derived from the study were informative. For instance, the average number of books owned by 10-year-old children in Austria was 23.57 (girls 24.9, boys 22.76). It was observed, however, that a significant correlation existed between the number of brothers and sisters and the number of books owned. The more siblings in the family, the fewer books owned. It is possible that an only child receives more books of his own. But it is also possible that the books owned in a larger family are considered community property and are read by all!

There is not adequate space to present all aspects of this study here. The complete report, available only in German, is well worth examination by interested persons.

Quite a different approach to research on what, why and how children read was adopted by the New Zealand Book Council which engineered an unusual project known as the 'Book Flood'.

Many investigators had become interested in the reason that some children had become habitual readers and others had not. However, no sustained and systematic experiment to test the assumption that reading tastes are likely to be influenced by the supply of books available had been conducted. For the research aspects of the Book Flood, the assistance of the New Zealand Centre for Educational Research was obtained. The Department of Education, the School Library Service and several advisory committees to plan the project in detail were also involved actively with the New Zealand Book Council.

The study was conducted in the city of Auckland, in which two primary schools had been identified by local inspectors as having enrolled many children who had limited access to books. Large numbers of Polynesian children from varying language backgrounds were in these schools. There were few books in their class-rooms, and the principals of the schools showed high interest in the project. Each school was to be supplied with 400–500 good books per class-room, from entering classes through the fourth standard, and the effects of this improved supply of books upon the reading habits, interests, and skills of children as well as the practices and views of the teachers were assessed. The experimenters pointed out the significant fact that the stack of books made available brought the collections available to these schools up to the range and quality of books available in the most favoured 10–15 per cent of schools of similar size and type.

A book selection committee comprised of several librarians, several principals who were assisted by librarians, and book-sellers with a thorough knowledge of children's books had the difficult task of selecting the books. They chose almost 10,000 titles, two-thirds of which were paperbacks and most of which were fiction, and ordered them in duplicate sets of up to six in each school. About 40 per cent were for junior school children, 40 per cent for below-average children in the middle school, and 20 per cent for the older, brighter pupils. The 350 books provided for each class-room, added to the 150 books already available, brought each class-room collection up to about 500 volumes.

Funds for book purchase came primarily from the New Zealand Book Trade Organization, with smaller gifts from the New Zealand Educational Institute, the New Zealand *Herald*, and the National Commission for Unesco. Several publishers supplied books at greatly reduced prices. Additional books were provided by the School Library Service, and the Auckland Education Board supplied the necessary book shelves. Parents and teachers from the schools sorted and catalogued the books.

The project was begun in the class-rooms before all the books had arrived, assuring a continual supply of new books, and a formal launching ceremony with appropriate publicity and a social gathering was held.

The initial impact of the 'Book Flood', according to informal observation by teachers and visitors, was good. The children seemed enthusiastic about the unaccustomed range of attractive and interesting books, and spent more time reading books and talking about them, borrowed more for home use, and took books home for their parents' reading. However, the investigators were not satisfied with these observations, for they do not tell us about the long-term effects of books on children's behaviour.

The Evaluation Committee selected and devised suitable tests, questionnaires and rating scales. Initial baseline levels for reading comprehension, vocabulary and listening skills were obtained, and a survey of reading interests was adapted to assess the children's interest in books and other reading materials. An attitude scale was used to assess the older children's attitudes toward school, reading, and themselves. The junior children's word recognition skills, letter identification, and familiarity with books and print were estimated with standardized tests and teacher-ratings on a three-point scale were used to assess the attitudes of the younger children. In addition, the teachers who participated made confidential assessments of their own practices and beliefs in the teaching of reading, using a check-list devised by the Evaluation Committee. All of these evaluations were made before the books were made available, so that follow-up comparisons could be made after the 'Book Flood' had been in operation for some time.

An intensive case-study was made of five children from each class. Questions were asked about books owned and read, home background, parental interest, library borrowing, television viewing, and other factors likely to be influenced by the 'Book Flood'. Studies were made of the children's reading behaviour, using informal reading inventories and running records.

From the baseline data, it was seen that in the life of the typical child in these schools, books and reading played a very small part. Few children had favourite authors, and most had little access to books. The average number of children in the families represented in the study was 5. The average child watched television for 22.5 hours per week, although some claimed over 47 hours of viewing. There were few books in the home, and in one school 81 per cent claimed that their parents never read to them. In the other school, the proportion was 44 per cent. More than half of the children never read a newspaper. The vast majority spoke English at home, but for many of them it was not their mother tongue.

After six months, the first measurements of the impact of 'Book Flood' were taken. The logs kept by children were evaluated and some were eliminated because they were apparently inflated. The statistical results bore out the observations of the teachers: the average child read 25 per cent more books, a difference which was statistically significant, and not due to chance.

The largest improvements were in listening comprehension. The evaluators, in their interim assessment, suggested, 'Apparently the extra time spent by teachers in reading aloud to their children from high-interest books, had a quick and measurable effect' [5]. Reading test scores were not so quickly changed, however, especially since the children, on average, read significantly below the national norm and many had serious problems derived from their bilinguality. The post-test scores were higher in fourteen of the twenty schools, and no loss in class score was greater than 0.5 points.

There were favourable shifts in attitude towards reading, but in only one school were these large enough to be considered statistically significant. No changes in self-concept were found in either school as a result of the Book Flood. Interest in reading was low to start, and remained low when the children rated their three preferred interests. Sports, television, art and 'going to the pictures' remained more interesting than reading. A previous sampling in Wellington had indicated that the public library was the main source of books, and the school library was third or fourth. Almost without exception, the pupils in the Book Flood schools saw school libraries as their main source of books, and the public libraries as third, fourth, or fifth out of six possible sources.

Promoting reading

Two other tendencies are worth noting. The Book Flood children tended to shift in their fiction choices from cowboy, war, and fairy stories to mystery and detective stories. There was also a trend towards selecting books on the basis of discussions with friends and teachers: the children talked more to friends about the books that interested them. Enid Blyton stories dropped from a position of highest popularity, giving way to Alfred Hitchcock, but few other pattern-changes in the choice of favourite authors were noted in the brief period included in the interim assessment. Similarly, there were only a few attitudinal changes among the teachers in the Book Flood schools.

One year later, additional measurements were taken to ascertain the long-term impact of the Book Flood. The children had more than doubled their reading as a result of the Flood. The reading and listening comprehension test results were very similar to those of the interim study. Listening comprehension improvement was the greatest, and the children, significantly in light of the nature of the group, held their own in the general skills measured by the reading tests. This is considered significant because children with language difficulties, and from depressed socio-economic and cultural conditions, often lose ground, rather than continue to gain, when compared with the general population. Other findings did not depart far from those obtained in the interim evaluation. This led to the conclusion that the Book Flood had marked effects during the first six months, and maintained these effects throughout the second year.

The teachers' views on the success of the experiment were varied, but the majority of the staff was confident that the project was successful in 'hooking' many children on books. It is interesting to observe that those teachers who reported a decline in interest in the Book Flood also revealed that the impact of the programme upon their own behaviour had been minimal.

In the final paragraph of the evaluation, the success of the Book Flood was summarized:

In sum, the majority of teachers felt that availability of a rich supply of 300–400 well-chosen books per classroom was a very commendable policy, and while not the critical factor in bringing children to a lasting habit of reading, it was an important first step. Their opinions are supported, by and large, with the information that most children were consistently reading much more, that their reading and listening skills were slowly but steadily improving and that they were becoming more familiar with books and authors.

Significantly, the National Book League in the United Kingdom has embarked on a long-term experiment along the same lines. The project is being funded by the British National Bibliography Research Fund Committee, and is being monitored by Bradford University's Postgraduate School of Studies in Research in Education, and will be followed with interest.

REFERENCES

1. SCHMIDCHEN, Gerhard. Lesekultur in Deutschland 1974. *Archiv fuer Sociologie und Wirtschaftsfragen des Buchhandels*, Vol. XXX, p. 707–896.
2. DE MEDINA, C. A.; DE ALMEIDA, M. L. Rodrigues. Habitos de Leitura: Uma Abordagem Sociologica. *Americas Latina*, Vol. XVII, 1976, p. 70–129.
3. BOSI, Eclea. *Cultura de Massa e Cultura Popular*. Petropolis, R.J. (Brasil), Editora Vozes, 1972. Sociological study of mass culture, focusing on the reading of workers in São Paulo.
4. BAMBERGER, Richard; BINDER, Lucia; VANECEK, Erich. *Zehnjährige als Buchleser*. Wien, Muenchen, Jugend und Volk, 1977.
5. ELLEY, W. B.; COWIE, C. R.; WATSON, J. E. *The Impact of Book Flood*, p. 10. Interim assessment prepared for the New Zealand Book Council. Wellington, New Zealand Centre for Educational Research, 1975.

The reading child

It is evident that one of the most effective ways of inculcating lifelong reading habits is to attract children to books and reading at the earliest possible age. Those concerned with reading promotion have thus evolved many kinds of special programmes aimed at young readers.

A small sampling of particularly innovative efforts will be presented here. Some relate to distribution, some to celebrations designed to call the attention of children to books, some with writing for children, book production, book awards and prizes, and others with the stimulation of reading through class-room activities, contests, and expanding the knowledge of adults who work with children about books and literature for children and young adults. There are many other children's book-promotion activities of a subtle and personal nature, engaged in by relatives, friends and peers with varying success. Since activities concentrated in libraries will be discussed in the following chapter, school and public library-oriented children's activities will not be included here.

SCHOOL BOOKSHOPS

Fostered by the National Book League, the British School Bookshop Association has gathered together an increasing number of the 4,000 bookshops in United Kingdom schools. The association promotes, publicizes, encourages and provides support for these bookshops; acts as a liaison between parents, teachers, booksellers and publishers; and serves as an information centre on all aspects of running a school bookshop.

The British school bookshop is just that, a real bookshop located within a school, but without the business worries of a commercial enterprise. A school may establish itself as a book agency, and can obtain books from a bookseller at a small discount on a sale or return basis after obtaining a license from the publishers' association for a small fee.

Since schools vary widely, each bookshop is designed to suit its own school's needs and circumstances, both in physical plant and in stock. Some are merely a locked cupboard; others are located in a large room used only for displaying and selling books. Any school may run its own bookshop from infants' schools to colleges.

The success of the British school bookshops in getting the children into the habit of buying books and becoming regular readers has been hailed by the book trade. The pleasure of choosing and buying from a wide range of books, conveniently located and without the solemnity of 'required reading' has appealed to many children, and has resulted in widespread support from educators, publishers and booksellers.

'JOY THROUGH BOOKS'

This is a French research and information organization which exists to develop lively relations between children and books. Open to librarians, teachers, parents, students, researchers and others who are interested in children's books, the Documentation and Research Centre contains works for children, French and foreign specialized books and magazines, dossiers and card catalogues on books, reading, libraries and pedagogy.

In addition to answering written and telephone inquiries, 'Joy Through Books' organizes meetings, conferences and training courses. It issues a bimonthly bulletin of information and criticism and a series of brochures for librarians.

Closely related to 'Joy Through Books' is an organization of some 500 writers, journalists, illustrators, publishers, critics, booksellers, teachers and librarians, called the Centre for Research and Information on Young People's Literature which made possible the French sponsorship of Hans Christian

Andersen Day in 1977. A commemorative poster chosen and published by the French Section of the International Board on Books for Young Children was widely distributed throughout the board's member countries.

THE ASIAN COPUBLICATION PROGRAMME

An example of international action that serves children and has many other spin-offs is the Asian Copublication Programme which has edited and published a series of 'Folktales from Asia' in fifteen languages in ten countries, and has also issued similar editions of the series 'Festivals from Asia'.

In addition to providing books for children, the production of this series is an exercise in multilingual and multicultural co-operation, and provides a training ground for printing, publishing and the distribution of books in the co-operating countries.

The first two books in the 'Folktales from Asia' series have been co-operatively issued in the following languages: Hindi, Indonesian, Javanese, Sundanese, Farsi, Japanese, Korean, Malay, Urdu, Chinese, English, Sinhalese, Tamil and Thai. The countries in which these books were issued include: India, Indonesia, Iran, Japan, the Republic of Korea, Malaysia, Pakistan, Singapore, Sri Lanka and Thailand.

Burma has also joined the co-operating countries. Although the printing of books for Burmese children started with a text-book in 1865 by missionaries, and some good books for children in Burmese were issued sporadically, they were not profitable, and were often of low quality.

The Asian Copublication Programme lent itself to the development of a high-quality Burmese children's book programme. It is a large step from translated comic books not adapted to local conditions to an edition of 10,000 copies of the folktales but the step has been taken and the Burmese children's book has now become a reality.

Book clubs and book weeks

Unique in many ways, the Austrian Book Club for Children has been a primary book promotion activity of the country for almost thirty years. Serving children from 3 to 18 years, it has developed from an enterprise with a small grant from the Ministry of Education, to a multifaceted book delivery, publishing, research, and publicity organization with a strong interest in how, why and what children read. The dedicated leadership of Dr Richard Bamberger and a fine staff have meant much to this organization.

The Minister of Education is the Honorary President of the club, and the managing committee consists of officials of organizations of an instructional or supervisory nature, teachers, and literary historians. The organization has the characteristics of a community service group. During the school year its programme provides lists of books from which choices can be made, and year-books for children, parents and teachers.

Support comes from the Ministry of Education, small individual dues (25 Austrian schillings per school year), contributions from parents and subventions from local governmental agencies. A lottery also provides funds for the purchase of books for school and class-room libraries. Co-operation comes from many sources, in addition to the Ministry of Education and the Arts. The entire school community, including teacher-education institutions, participates, as well as all Austrian publishers, booksellers, public and private libraries, editors of cultural journals, and parents' organizations.

At present there are about 700,000 paying members, who provide a substantial part of the income of the Book Club. This number does not include those children who are provided with free membership for philanthropic reasons. It is significant to note that the Book Club's most effective secretariat is not satisfied with the attention given to its activities by daily and weekly newspapers, as well as television coverage of the activities of the club.

Sponsored by the Japanese Council, as well as some other groups associated with newspapers and mass communication, is an annual Children's National Book Week. Under this umbrella are conducted a wide range of activities which encourage children to read, including children's book fairs, exhibitions of picture books from around the world, book report contests, and the wide distribution of a pamphlet recommending 100 good books for children.

AWARDS

Many awards have been made to authors, illustrators and others involved in the provision of books for children. The Children's Book Council in the United States of America, whose function is to promote children's books and reading, has found it necessary to issue a 198-page book biennially to list the awards given in the United States, the Commonwealth countries, and internationally [1]. These include the Hans Christian Andersen Award, the Bienniale of Illustrations Bratislava, the Bologna Children's Book Fair prizes and the International Board on Books for Young People Honour List. It is not possible to present information here about this fast-growing means of attracting attention to children's materials, and of rewarding those who are engaged in providing young people with the stimulation for a lifetime of reading. Perhaps it would be useful to mention one, however. Shoichi Noma, a leading Japanese publisher long interested in international publishing, was given the International Book Award in 1974 for his work for the international book community. In commemoration of this, he donated 10 million yen to the Asian Cultural Centre for Unesco, which established the Noma International Book Fund whose income will be used to promote the quality of children's picture books in developing countries, a great need for beginning readers. A contest of illustrations of children's picture books was to be held annually starting in 1978.

In Canada, Children's Literature Prizes were established by the Canada Council in 1975 to aid and encourage Canadian authors of books for young people. The prizes, worth $5,000 each, are awarded annually to one English-language and one French-language writer. Formal applications are not required as the six-member jury appointed by the council reviews all children's books published by Canadian authors during the calendar year, and the prize-winning titles are announced in May.

It should be added that recognition of the producers and consumers of children's books need not be on a grand scale to be effective. Writers enjoy meeting their audiences and often derive benefit from talking to small groups of students. Students and their families often treasure recognition for achievement.

INTERNATIONAL YOUTH LIBRARY

A public service agency serving the international children's book community, the International Youth Library in Munich, is financed by local government and private contributors. The library serves many functions in addition to displaying children's books from many publishing sources. It has, for instance, issued a *Directory of Correspondents* listing children's book experts throughout the world.

Recently, with the influx of *Gastarbeiter* (guest workers) and their children from many southern European countries and elsewhere, the library embarked on a many-sided programme to meet the reading needs of children and youth from immigrant families and other minorities. The library compiles and distributes check-lists of children's books in foreign languages for the families of migrant workers. The lists are used also by public libraries, schools, and factory libraries as a source of information about the best books available from more than sixty countries. Supplementary lists of current literature are available to update the 'best books', which are divided into four reading age groups. Titles are chosen on the basis of the reading tastes of immigrant children and their families, proven classics, works appreciated in the home countries, and books representing life and culture in the homeland. Lists of publishers' addresses and information about importing are also made available by the library. To further the exchange of knowledge, a series of workshops are being conducted, with representatives of the home country knowledgeable in the field participating, such as teachers, cultural attachés, social workers and radio specialists.

READING COMPETITIONS

The opening of Children's Book Week in the Federal Republic of Germany inaugurates an annual reading competition which is national in scope. Entrants from the sixth year of school select three-to-five minute texts to read aloud. They represent various kinds of schools, and opportunities are given to foreign-language children who have not been in the Federal Republic of Germany longer than four years as well as children from special schools for the retarded. Over 380,000 children participate in the oral-reading competition at the local level; winners go on to the State and then to the national level. The final decision is reached annually at the Goethe Haus in Frankfurt.

BUNKO: CHILDREN'S LIBRARIES IN JAPAN

Bunko is a Japanese word which literally means 'a storehouse of literature'. It is often used for a private collection of books. When the word is used in connection with children today, however, it refers to a small children's library sponsored by various non-governmental groups and individuals. In Japan, where public libraries are unfortunately not yet well developed, these small private libraries in the area of children's reading have an important role to play and are gaining considerable influence over the total sphere of children and books in the country.

A *bunko* originated in private homes. A person, often a housewife who is interested in sharing her love of books with children in her neighbourhood, invites them to her house, usually once a week in the afternoon. She then offers them her collection of children's books which they can either take home to read or have read to them. This is just one step ahead of lending one's own books to personal friends with whom one wants to share the pleasure of reading.

Promoting reading

Such a library run by an individual is called *katei bunko*, or a home library, and came into being in the country about twenty years ago. The idea caught the attention of many adults who were concerned with children's reading, and by people volunteered to sponsor such a library in their neighbourhood.

Writers of children's books, who naturally have a large collection, began to offer their books to children. It was a good way for them to have first-hand knowledge of how children respond to books.

Older housewives, whose children had outgrown their collection of children's books and who were left with some leisure time, picked up the idea. It served to keep them occupied and gave them the satisfaction of working for others, especially for growing children.

Meanwhile, the younger housewives, whose growing children were in urgent need of good reading materials, were also drawn to the idea. Those young mothers got together and formed a group. Each contributed a small sum of money with which they jointly purchased books to be circulated among their children. It was the beginning of a co-operative effort to provide children with good books. When such a group was formed in a large government housing area, for example, instead of having the collection in a private home, they placed it in the community centre, thus giving the library more of a public character.

A library that was no longer located in the home, nor the management purely personal, was called *chiiki bunko*, or a community library. Though called by that it was financed by concerned individuals and managed by their voluntary services.

Soon kindergartens and nursery schools began to develop libraries, which were called *en bunko*, or a kindergarten library. Christian churches and Buddhist temples joined in the movement and started small libraries of their own for children who came to their Sunday schools.

Thus interest in *bunko* and children's reading has grown all over the country and, as a result, the development of public libraries was accelerated. The new public libraries make it a point to serve children and when they have a budget for books but not for personnel, they even try to encourage mothers to open a *bunko*, promising to provide the necessary books for them. Such libraries that are publicly supported but privately run will grow as service points of the public library and, in fact, there were cases where the efforts of mothers earned a branch library in their community.

It is said that there are about 4,000 *bunko* of various kinds throughout the country now. It is interesting to note that the number is seven times that of public libraries which render services to children.

This idea of a small private library for children seems to fascinate many people outside Japan who share an interest in children and books. It naturally appealed to people in whose countries public libraries are yet to be developed, for this is something they can start themselves and yet it has the potential to become a stimulus for children—to motivate them to read—as well as adults—to let them realize the need for good books and libraries for children.

Although the increase of such private libraries for children will not be the final solution to the various problems concerning children and books in Japan, the idea can very effectively be applied to some countries as the first step towards betterment of children's books and libraries.

PARENT-CHILD READING

Another movement which has spread all over Japan was begun in 1960 by Hatoju Muku in Kagoshima Prefecture. In this plan, children read aloud from a book for twenty minutes every day while their parents (usually mothers) listen to them. This simple plan has the advantage of having the parent and child share the same feelings and obtain the same knowledge through reading a book. It is also effective in promoting the reading habit.

Another similar plan encourages mothers to read aloud to their infants and young children, even though little comprehension of what is read takes place. The psychological effect of such reading creates warmth and positive attitudes towards books and reading which are difficult to duplicate in later life.

In rural areas, it was found that the main reason for non-reading is the lack of availability of books at home. To combat this situation, a 'one-book-in-every-home movement' was organized by several schools and libraries in rural areas. In Nagano Prefecture, schoolchildren served as book distributors, delivering books from the library to the homes of people in the district. In Kagoshima, local libraries sent at least one book to each home. In Yatsuchiro, the library delivered one book to each home. It is important to know that in these three instances, books were *not* lent in response to a request. Nevertheless, the 'one-book-in-every-home movement' was found to have motivated book reading in children and adults.

REFERENCES

1. Children's Book Council. *Children's Books: Awards and Prizes.* New York, N.Y., The Children's Book Council. 67 Irving Place, New York, N.Y. 10003, 1977. Biennial publication listing.

Library outreach

All libraries foster the use and appreciation of books and
reading. They do it in different ways, however. The private
library which serves a restricted clientele—members of the
family—obviously will not affect as many potential readers as
an open, public library. Similarly, the public library which
actively seeks to attract readers, to stimulate them into borrowing, reading and talking about books is likely to have more
influence than a formidable fortress which repels, rather than
attracts, readers.

But if there are no libraries at all, discussion of differences
among libraries is merely academic. Libraries which have sufficient human and financial resources to serve the needs of
those who have 'book hunger' should be a foundation stone
in the development of a nation. Through Unesco, materials
which will aid in the planning of national information systems
are available. Both a basic set of objectives for national and
international action [1] and recommendations for establishing a
legislative framework for the implementation of National Information Systems [2] have been published by Unesco. These
show how books—even very short books—can provide time-
and money-saving services.

Mutual exchange of information and experiences about
similar problems is also beneficial. This type of exchange can
take place in a seminar such as that described by Fonotov [3]
organized in the Union of Soviet Socialist Republics and
financed by Unesco. One enthusiastic reporter commented that
the seminar demonstrated the importance of books and other
sources of information in the developing countries, the growing

interest felt by the peoples of these countries in the establishment of libraries, and the progress which had been achieved
in library development. It would not be possible to describe
all—or even a small proportion of the contributions of libraries
and librarians to reading. Just a few of them will be touched
upon. Outstanding examples of library promotion in several
countries, a description of how one country promotes the use
of libraries, and some ways in which libraries have helped
our understanding of readers will be described.

'EL BANCO DEL LIBRO'

Since 1960, the 'Banco del Libro' movement has been leading
the way in the development of Venezuela's libraries. It was
started by a group of volunteers under the leadership of
Virginia Betancourt, who was awarded the 1978 International
Book Award for her efforts over the years. Initially, the Banco
del Libro was concerned with the provision of reading materials
to children and youth, but it has grown greatly in its aspirations
and activities [4].

It has since won the confidence of many people, has been
recognized by the National Library which has designated the
Banco del Libro as the provider of technical services to the public
libraries and has provided much assistance to the Ministry of
Education in its library activities. The Banco has sponsored
a system of public libraries in Caracas, a network of school
libraries in Ciudad Guayana, a training centre for librarians,
a documentation centre for library service and education.

In 1969, a network of bookmobiles was started to extend the
library services of Caracas, which now provides 100,000 users
with access to books annually, especially children and youths
in outlying areas. The system is carefully designed around a
central library, with satellite library buildings in communities.

In Ciudad Guayana, an important commercial centre,
school libraries were organized to serve 62 public schools,
with 35,000 students and 900 teachers. In 1973, this programme
led the Ministry of Education to recognize the programme
as one which has contributed to the formation of the reading

habit, to the development of children's curiosity and desire to search for information, and to provide intellectual development.

Although the Banco del Libro was founded to provide children with books, it also considers the distribution of a broad spectrum of materials, including the classics and a large selection of Latin American literature. It is a fine example of volunteers providing leadership in the building of an outstanding permanent institution.

KOREAN VILLAGE MINI-LIBRARIES

For several years the Korean Library Association has asked the government to revise the Library Act of 1963, now out of date, so as to give financial support to the improvement of libraries, and to help alleviate the shortage of librarians. But even before the 1963 Library Act was passed, a movement had begun to provide books for the village people in rural areas.

In 1960, the Korean Mini-library Association started its activities. It was made up of volunteers, and was incorporated a year later as a non-profit organization. The original purpose of the movement was to furnish fishing and rural villages with standard book cabinets containing an initial collection of twenty to thirty books chosen by the villagers. By February 1977, 35,011 mini-libraries had been established, and 2,848,433 books were listed in their holdings.

The office of the association, which is located in Seoul (Republic of Korea), contains only several tables and chairs, and employs seven regular workers, including three professional librarians. Although the association has no fixed source of funds, it nevertheless has had great nation-wide influence. Contributions from individuals, companies, social organizations and local governments have paid for its expenses and operation.

Each village mini-library is started by a reading club composed of about ten young people who lead the movement in their home village. The village mini-library is actually operated by this reading club. In 1977, there were 497,813 members, who received a monthly four-page paper, the *Maul-Munko* (Village Mini-library) for their subscription fee of the equivalent of $20 per year. This newspaper has been issued since 1964. In 1975, the association began to put greater emphasis on the quality of the holdings in each village.

It is significant that the initiator of this grass-roots movement, Dae-sup Ohm, was a librarian who had established a privately supported public library in his home town in 1951. While he was serving as director of this library, he had begun sending books to villages. When he became the Korean Library Association's first executive director, he continued to carry on this 'used-books-sending movement'. Without bookcases and reading clubs to organize lending activities, the books sent to villages were not utilized, and so the movement was not successful.

Now, the autonomous reading clubs, which are responsible for the operation, management and development of the mini-libraries, not only conduct business but also meet for discussion about books which members have read. Members within a certain community may hold meetings to exchange books, ideas and personal experiences. Mini-libraries also exchange books with other libraries, and serve as branches and deposit stations of public libraries, which loan a certain number of books within their community areas on a long-term basis for circulation to villages.

The brochure which the Korean Village Mini-library has issued includes a significant comment:

Most developing countries are not yet at a stage to invest for library development, mainly because they are pressed with national economic development activities, while the developed countries are able to establish many public libraries for people to use. Therefore, it is desirable in developing countries that people themselves make efforts to develop a reading movement in order to claim their civil right to read. The VML movement starts from the grass roots with the people and eventually can stimulate the establishment of public libraries [5].

BOX LIBRARIES IN PAKISTAN

A demand by villagers and slum dwellers with only rudimentary education led to the development in Pakistan of a wooden box of about 100 Urdu books, which came to be known as the portable or Elementary Box Library. Popular demand for more sophisticated materials by people with more education but no access to Urdu books led to the development of the Advanced Box Library.

Support for the project came from the Asia Foundation, which has made available more than 1,100 elementary box libraries, assembled on five different occasions. In addition, 150 advanced box libraries were collected and distributed. The box libraries are provided to community and voluntary organizations after requests have been screened so that duplication of already-existing library facilities will be avoided, and so as to guarantee that the recipient organization is capable of adding to the collections through local support.

FARM LIBRARIES

About 15,000 farmers now have their own home libraries as the result of a plan organized by the University of Agriculture at Lyallpur (Pakistan) to provide up-to-date information about good farm practices. Farmers who pay 5 rupees annually become members of the Farm Library Registry, and receive extension bulletins on such subjects as methods of producing better crops, plant protection measures, livestock management, etc. There are already 120 such bulletins available with 60 more in preparation, and the university plans to issue a total of 300 dealing with all aspects of agriculture, and is currently involved in the production of literacy textbooks and post-literacy materials, including pamphlets on subjects of interest to newly literate women [6].

While this programme is primarily directed towards the dissemination of agricultural information, perhaps it will serve as a foundation for the encouragement of home libraries of a more general nature when the time is right.

'READING IS FUNDAMENTAL'

Starting with volunteers, accumulating support from professionals and the United States Government, 'Reading is Fundamental' (RIF) is dedicated to inexpensive book distribution in schools and libraries in the United States. It is headed by Margaret MacNamara, who has been the driving force behind the movement since the beginning.

Although books are given to children gratis, local funds pay part of the cost, usually raised through the activities of volunteer agencies and individuals.

The RIF programme has been compared to seed-sowing. Library borrowing rises after children have been given their own books to take home, for in those cases in which books are a scarce commodity, the gift book sows the seed of future growth in reading. The joy of seeing a child receiving his own book has repaid many community volunteers for their time and energy.

FINLAND'S SUCCESS STORY

Generous State support, a well-planned policy, and the country's best architects have been combined to make Finland's public library system one of the most successful in the world. Annual library loans average nine books per capita, and one-third of the population is a library member.

The growth of public libraries—each of Finland's 518 communes has one, and there are 2,600 annexes and 140 bookmobiles which serve the rural areas—has been phenomenal. The 1962 law places no ceiling on State financial aid and provides financial assistance in proportion to each library's actual expenses. Subventions range from 90 per cent for hospital libraries, two-thirds of real expenditures for rural communal libraries and one-third for urban communal libraries.

The librarians are free to choose the books purchased, but must keep in mind that the library public has diversified tastes. Specialized collections are located where they are appropriate. In the town of Rovaniemi, for instance, the population of 26,000 has a library covering 3,000 square metres, has lending services for adults, adolescents and children, a language laboratory and a collection of 5,000 volumes on the Lapps and Lapland. Some 250,000 volumes are borrowed each year.

Some of the best Finnish architects have designed the

libraries, selecting colours and furnishings which give each library its own personality. This makes Finnish libraries aesthetically attractive and inviting. The library law has also provided financial support for the authors of books—a sum representing 5 per cent of total authorized credits is allocated to writers.

LIBRARY USAGE

Almost all library governing boards are concerned about the impact of their institution, and collect evidence on the number of patrons and the number of books circulated. Many libraries have gone far beyond the collection of rudimentary data of this type, and have studied their patrons' needs and aspirations. This is desirable and even necessary. Schools of Library Science have sponsored many studies of this nature.

In Hungary, the library community has been particularly active in this respect. In 1977, the journal *Konyvtari Figuelo* devoted a special issue [7] to reading research, and a number of publications have been issued on various aspects of library effectiveness [8, 9], and the effect of a novel on readers [10], or the literary value of the reading done by a sampling of patrons [11]. A summary in English of the reading research done from 1968 to 1977 in the National Széchényi Library Centre for Library Science has been published by the library [12].

In Africa, a librarian who was an official of the Institut Panafricain pour le Développement [13] made an observation study of the typology of readers and public libraries of West Africa. Having worked as a librarian in English-speaking and French-speaking countries in Africa for fifteen years, the author had access to records and librarians in all of western Africa.

The classification of readers using public libraries was made into: (a) 'bulimic readers', who read voraciously for no utilitarian purpose, (b) 'swotters', who read mainly in order to cram for an examination, and (c) 'information foragers', who read only occasionally and to seek specific information, usually in their particular form of work. Although the 'bulimic' readers do not make much use of the libraries available in western

Africa, the demands of the other two groups have expended the limited available resources in ways that have prevented the development of school-like or balanced libraries. The observer suggests that western African libraries have provided an extremely low-cost service, but that future support must come from each national budget. However useful foreign or international aid may be, the national authorities alone can ensure the development of a truly national service.

REFERENCES

1. *Objectives for National and International Action.* Paris, Unesco, 1975. 30 p.
2. *Establishing a Legislative Framework for the Implementation of Natis.* Paris, Unesco, 1977.
3. FONOTOV, G. P. Seminar of Librarians from Asia, Africa and Latin America in the USSR. *Unesco Bulletin for Libraries,* Vol. XXX, March–April 1976, p. 101–3.
4. EL BANCO DEL LIBRO. Una Ejemplar Institución Cultural Venezolana. *Noticias del Centro Regional para el Fomento del Libro en América Latina,* No. 15, 1–16 September 1977, p. 8–9.
5. *Village Mini-library Movement in Korea,* p. 4. Seoul (Republic of Korea), Korean Mini-Library Association. (Pamphlet.)
6. HUSSEIN, Ghulam. Farm Library Scheme. *Literacy Documentation,* Vol. VI, No. 1, 1977, p. 1–6.
7. *Könyvtári Figeló* az OKDT es a KMK Folyoirata, 1977, p. 3–4.
8. HALÁSZ, László; NAGY, Attila. *Hatásvizsgálat Könyvtárban I.* Budapest, Nepmuvelesi Propaganda Iroda, 1974.
9. HALASZ, Lászlo; NAGY, Attila. *Hatásvizsgálat Könyvtárban II.* Budapest, Nepmuvelesi Propaganda Iroda, 1977.
10. KAMARÁS, István; KISS, Endre; SOMORJAI, Ildiko. *A 'Makra' Es 116 Olvasoja.* Budapest, 1977.
11. KAMARÁS, István. *Az Irodalmi Érték Esélye Lektürol Vasóknál.* Budapest, Nepmuvelesi Propaganda Iroda, 1974.
12. NATIONAL SZECHENYI LIBRARY. *Reading Research in the Centre for Library Science and Methodology.* Budapest, National Szechenyi Library, 1977.
13. LALANDE-ISNARD, Fanny. Typology of Readers and of Public Libraries in West Africa. *Unesco Bulletin of Libraries,* Vol. XXXI, September–October 1977, p. 292–331.

Evaluating the evidence

The descriptions in the previous chapters may lead one to draw conclusions about activities in book promotion. It must be emphasized that the descriptions are not complete, nor have they all been evaluated critically. Almost all had their local critics.

It can be seen that many ways to encourage the use of reading and books have been used; here we will attempt some generalizations about them, dangerous as that may be. This summary will inevitably leave out some of the useful generalizations. It is hoped, however, that it will point the way to some activities which readers can adapt in their own situations, or which they can use as a background for the new, creative activities which they will devise.

There appears to be little doubt that reading can be encouraged. In those instances in which careful evaluation was conducted, the evidence is clear. The book hunger which Barker and Escarpit have described [1] exists, and while it is extravagant to think that every literate person can be made into an avid reader, there are many ways in which the proportion of the population who actively read can be increased.

In those countries in which the provision of reading materials, and the encouragement to use them, have become a high priority of the government and the private sector, the results have been good and one thing has become evident: effort on the part of the community is necessary if change is to occur in the reading public's size and enthusiasm for buying or borrowing books. The book community, which includes publishers of all kinds of materials, booksellers and other distribution outlets, governments, writers and translators, as well as librarians and educators, can produce striking results if they will plan and work together. This is not an area in which we can 'let someone else do it'.

It is also clear that distribution is a problem. The movement of books from publishers to readers often encounters serious obstacles. This is especially true in countries where the distribution of all goods is a problem. In some cases, an evaluation and revision of the system itself is required. In other cases, more effective use of existing facilities and practices is called for, and modification is much easier.

An efficient postal system has proved to be an important agency, although the personal advice service which is part of a good bookstore, and is missing in mail-order purchases, can be very useful to a literate person who needs help in knowing about and using the wealth of materials potentially available in any bookstore.

We have also seen that libraries are a major factor in successfully promoting the reading habit. A well-stocked library can be the means by which an individual can step into the world of books and partake of its riches. Part of the service of such a library is the advice of a considerate librarian, whose help in locating materials, encouraging a shy reader, and stimulating a patron to go on to more and better information is invaluable. It is significant that trained librarians are usually leaders in movements in which greater numbers of people are reached—the so-called 'library outreach' activities. They have often fostered 'box libraries' of various kinds in which poorly housed and poorly staffed 'libraries' build interest in the advantages of books and their informative delights. Libraries provide services in many ways, and different levels of libraries—from the most primitive to the most specialized—offer much of value to the clientele they serve.

One function of libraries which may easily be overlooked is that of providing financial support to the publishing industry. Although a library may purchase only one copy of a book for lending purposes, where there are 500 libraries, the guaranteed sale of 500 copies may enable a publisher to make the decision that he will not go out of business if he issues the publication. We should not forget that Gutenberg himself died bankrupt, working as a servant. In some countries, royalties are paid to authors for library copies sold, a further encouragement to the writer. Governments have encouraged national publishing by purchasing books for schools and libraries out of public funds.

One of the deterrents to acquiring the reading habit is simply that books are often expensive. New readers—those who are newly literate, or who have just learned about the values and delights of reading—are likely to be poor. Newspapers, magazines and other inexpensive publications are not *objets d'art* as are some lavishly illustrated, attractively printed and artistically bound museum pieces, but they provide the availability—and the practice—needed to build the reading habit. When books are priced out of the buyer's reach, the size of the market diminishes. Every effort should be made to keep the cost of reading materials at a reasonable level.

Books as gifts are popular, and have been used to start a child on the road to reading and, presumably, book collecting. Books given as prizes do the same. If a book is earned, or there is a reason for its being a gift, it is apparently more likely to be appreciated than if it falls from heaven. There is no evidence, however, that book giveaways create sustained readers.

International efforts and in particular the activities connected with International Book Year 1972 provide many sources of information about book-related projects. The 'Programme of Action' developed for IBY '72 has many suggestions which may serve as a point of departure for book and reading promotion activities and is worth examining, as are the newsletters issued by Unesco and various regional agencies—*Book Promotion News*, the *Newsletter of the Tokyo Book Development Centre*, the *Newsletter of the Asian Book Development Centre* in Karachi, and the newsletter of the Centro Regional para el Fomento del Libro en América Latina. In addition, Unesco's 'Reports and Papers on Mass Communication' series and its many periodicals and publications regarding libraries and librarianship are valuable.

As has been pointed out, readership studies are essential

to know what potential readers do with their time, and what they are interested in reading about. Studies done in related fields of social science can tell us about the needs and desires of the reading public and the potential reading public. Information about the market they serve is important to the publisher and bookseller as a basic business tool. Information about their clientele for purposes of best being of service to them, is important to libraries and librarians.

Since the best readership studies are sophisticated scientific studies, and since the interpretation of statistical data is treacherous for amateurs, a word of caution should be raised about using readership studies with care. We would not try to interpret X-ray negatives without help from a physician, who often depends upon a specialist. We should not interpret statistical data without help from a statistician or other specialist who carefully examines the total picture.

A case may prove the point. In the previously mentioned study of the reading of Austrian 10-year-olds one question is how many books a child owns. The researchers point out that results should take into account that in large families books are not always considered one child's property, but are read by all and are, in reality, family property. A realistic, analytical mind with experience in dealing with questionnaire data is necessary when interpreting readership studies. It is difficult to measure some characteristics, such as attitudes, and usually it is impossible, in one questionnaire, to pin down shifts in interests that can be reflected in book selection choices. A series of studies which provide comparative data is often necessary.

A number of readership studies conducted in various countries were not described in pages 61–9. They are indicated here because of their potential usefulness by planners. First should be mentioned an annotated bibliography of studies called *The Reading Habits of Adults* by Margaret Mann. It is the first British National Bibliography Research Fund Report, and includes 609 studies [2].

As examples of readership studies not previously mentioned, it is useful to cite those done in Benin [3], Norway [4, 5], Spain [6], and Sri Lanka [7]. The first was prepared by the

Evaluating the evidence

National Commission for Unesco of Benin; the Norwegian reports (one is a summary of a comprehensive report) were made for the Norwegian Book Club; and the Spanish study was made by the National Institute for Statistics. Data on Flemish youth were sketched by Frans Schittecat of Belgium using information provided by the Association for the Promotion of Flemish Books and the services for the supply of reading by the Ministry of Dutch Culture [8].

A survey of the reading tastes of children and young persons in Sri Lanka was made at the suggestion of the Unesco Regional Centre for Book Development in Asia. The study was very objective, and dealt with 7,088 Sinhala-speaking and 1,567 Tamil-speaking children.

The importance of early reading has been confirmed. Reading starts in the parent's lap, say the Japanese. Most authorities agree that the best way to develop a reading population is by educating children to become readers. Schools and libraries are unusually co-operative in working with reading promotion activities for children.

Children's books can be promoted through special means, which are often not appropriate for adults. Competitions are popular. One American charity, the National Multiple Sclerosis Society, raised U.S.$7 million through a 'MS Read-a-thon'. In this competition, sponsors in the community agree to pay the charity a fixed sum such as a few cents or a dollar for each book read by a child. Both the child who reads and the charity's research fund benefit from this programme.

Reading also stimulates writing and thinking on the part of students. Good teachers have long taken advantage of every possible means of encouraging the growth of students in every direction. Some systematic approaches to the ways in which children can be motivated to read have been published. One collection of activities for schools was collected and published by the Utah Council of the International Reading Association [9], and a fine collection devoted to story-telling in libraries was issued by the American Library Association [10]. There are many approaches to bringing books and children together.

Mention must also be made of the importance of proper co-ordination in carrying out book-and-reading promotion activities. If a National Book Development Council exists, it is a likely place to find the leadership which is so necessary. It is useful—indeed, essential—to devise a detailed plan, so that the greatest effect can be realized. The leadership should be prepared to make adjustments in case of unexpected developments, both good and bad.

One way in which book promotion can lose its effectiveness is if it appears to be commercial. Selling books is the ultimate object of many reading campaigns, but it should not be so obvious to the public that all pleasure is driven away. On the other hand, a sophisticated campaign can attract the attention of many persons, but there is no evidence that it makes sustained book readers out of them.

Outside consultants are very useful, especially in pointing out new and different ways in which a promotion can be carried out. Consultants should not be depended upon to do the work of the book industry, however. If they are engaged to plan and carry out a programme, they will need the support of the book world, including the industry members, who sometimes tend to sit back and watch the consultants perform instead of pitching in with whole-hearted support. The book community at large is remarkably willing to enter into book-promotion activities. International Book Year 1972 was counted successful far beyond expectation because of the support it received world-wide, often from unexpected sources.

After a project has been completed, it is especially useful to have someone critically and unemotionally evaluate it. The rosy glow of a successful campaign needs to be analysed if a similar programme is planned for the future. The time to evaluate is soon after the closing—not when everyone is exhausted from working at fever pitch for a period of time as it is difficult to be unemotional at that time—but before time has taken its toll. Memory is short. One week after closing is usually a good time to evaluate a programme for future planning purposes. The leader of the evaluation team should do everything possible to keep recriminations, bitterness, and blame off the evaluation agenda. Building for the future requires a positive foundation.

Governments can provide aid in many ways. The political leadership should not be overlooked in planning book-promotion activities. Local and provincial officials, as well as national leaders, are in a position to lend support and also to derive political stature from participating in book-promotion activities. National libraries are also a natural base of support for book activities for they can be used for displays, and their distribution facilities are often excellent.

Privately supported programmes are also useful. Associations of publishers and booksellers are involved in many programmes. Foundations can often provide impetus which would otherwise be lacking in promotion programmes. But they are rarely willing to grant permanent support to programmes, authors, for book production, or for minority language publishing. These are the functions, they say, of governments.

Finally, there is no substitute for dedicated leadership in book-promotion activities. Influencing change is a long-term process and women like Virginia Betancourt in Venezuela, Margaret MacNamara in the United States, as well as men like Richard Bamberger in Austria have given much of themselves to the cause of providing materials for children's reading. Volunteer workers often start action, and use their influence to accomplish things which would otherwise not take place. (A summary of how the great energy of volunteers can be harnessed is *Getting People to Read* which tells about programmes in the United States [11].) A mix of volunteer leadership and government support is a happy combination in carrying out large-scale programmes, and in many countries, leadership can be found outside the ranks of book professionals.

What is clear is that plans for the programme should be made meticulously, with the active involvement of those who will do the actual work once the project gets under way.

The organizers of a book-and-reading promotion activity have many options, many of which have been described in the preceding pages. Success is more likely if the people involved are concerned about the success of the venture, no matter what activity is planned. Those who have major responsibilities should be carefully chosen.

A second requirement is that a clear picture of the situation be obtained. Not only should the reading status of the population involved be studied, but also its activity patterns, educational and economic status, and library use. All of these are related to the likelihood of success. A full-scale readership study is desirable, when possible.

Not only is this type of information necessary, but the organizers should have a clear idea of the facilities and media which are available. Sources of this information are often available through commercial or government channels. Exhibits cost money to erect, and exhibitors must be willing to show their wares. Getting the facts about the potential audience, all the accessible facilities, the costs, and the availability of support is essential to the success of any promotion.

Assessing the situation on the basis of the facts is the next step, and is one which can save much time and energy, because it is likely to eliminate unprofitable activities. Plans should include the activities preceding, during and following the venture, for all are important. Announcements and other publicity before the event are essential, for without an audience, a play cannot be performed. Every possible eventuality should be anticipated. There will always be some which will be overlooked, and adjustments can easily be made.

The plans should also include examining the project after it is completed, to learn what appears to be successful in your situation, and what has failed. Failures should be analysed, too, to learn how they can be overcome. A written report is a great aid to the human memory, and a useful way to enlist support for the next campaign. It also permits those who follow to profit from previous successes.

REFERENCES

1. BARKER, Ronald; ESCARPIT, Robert. *The Book Hunger*. Paris, Unesco, 1973.
2. MANN, Margaret. *The Reading Habits of Adults*. A Selected

Annotated Bibliography. London, British Library, Sheraton House, Great Chapel Street, London W1V 4BH, 1977. (British National Bibliography Research Report No. 1.)

3. Ministère de l'Enseignement du Premier Degré. *Enquête sur la Lecture en République du Bénin*. Porto-Novo, Bénin, Commission Béninoise pour l'Unesco, 1977.

4. NORENG, Øystein. *Lesign og Kommunikasjon*. Kort Rapport om Den Norske Bokklubbens Lesersociologiske Undersøkelse. Oslo, Den Norske Bokklubbens, 1974.

5. NORENG, Øystein. *Lesere og Lesing*. Rapport om Den Norske Bokklubbens Lesersociologiske Undersøkelse. Oslo, Den Nordiske Bokklubbens, 1974.

6. INSTITUTO NACIONAL DE ESTADÍSTICA. *Encuestade Habitos de Lectura*. Madrid, Instituto Nacional de Estadística, 1976.

7. WEERASURIYA, D. S. *A Report on the Survey of Reading Tastes of Children and Young People in Sri Lanka*. Columbo, Educational Publications Department.

8. SCHITTICAT, Frans. Flemish Youth and the Book. *Bookbird*, No. 4, 1977.

9. UTAH COUNCIL, INTERNATIONAL READING ASSOCIATION. *Motivating Interest in Reading*. Salt Lake City, Utah, March 1971.

10. BAUER, Caroline Feller. *Handbook for Storytellers*. Chicago, Ill., American Library Association, 1977.

11. SMITH, Carl, B.; FAY, Leo C. *Getting People to Read*. New York, Delacorte Press, 1973. 238 p.

Appendix 1
Motivation for reading:
an international bibliography[1]

The following bibliography was compiled with the help of the International Book Committee, an inter-professional body of book experts closely associated with Unesco's Book Development Programme.

Items for the bibliography were found in many places. The normal available bibliographic tools were used in a library search, and the Educational Resources Information Center of the National Institute of Education in the United States was searched for items published, using the descriptors, 'reading habits', 'reading interests', 'reading behaviour', and 'recreational reading'.

Special thanks are due to Ms Yasuko Wakabayashi of Heibonsha Limited, Publishers, for translating the Japanese references into English. The references are published, of course, in the Japanese language, even though they appear in English in this bibliography.

A decision which affects the quality of the bibliography was made when it was found that it was not possible to annotate all of the citations. Rather than discard those entries for which no annotation was possible, it was decided to provide as much information as was available, namely, a reference. A descriptive title may be useful in directing the reader to a publication of interest; omitting the title completely would be of no help whatever.

The bibliographic style varies according to the sources from which the entries were taken and custom in the country of origin. Whenever possible, entries are presented as they appeared in source materials.

1. Compiled by Ralph C. Staiger, International Reading Association.

ITEMS PUBLISHED IN 1973-74

ANGYAL, Erzsébet. A Könyv a Modern Társadalom Fejlödésében. *Könyvtári Figyelö*, Vol. 20, 3 S2, 1974, p. 249-58.
The book in the development of modern society. Lectures given in an international seminar in Belgrade, April 1973.

ARIAS, Gloria Nieto de, *et al. Qué Leer*. Bogotá, Editorial Universitaria de América, 1975.

ASKOV, Eunice N.; TISCHBACK, Thomas J. An Investigation of Primary Pupils' Attitudes towards Reading. *Journal of Experimental Education*, Vol. 41, spring 1973, p. 1-7.
Askov's Primary Pupil Reading Attitude Inventory and the Stanford Achievement Tests were administered to seventy-five first- and ninety-five third-grade children to investigate relationships between attitudes towards reading and achievement, sex and grade placement. The stability of attitude scores over time was also studied. Results indicate that attitude was significantly related to the paragraph meaning but not to the word reading subtests of the Stanford Achievement Test. Attitude scores were significantly higher for the seventy-five females than the ninety-five males. Grade level was not significantly related to attitude when achievement was held constant. Attitude scores remained stable from spring to autumn.

BÁLINT-LEHEL, Tamásné; NÁNDORNÉ, Hargitai. *Mit Olvasnak 1936 —Ban és 1969—Ben a 3. Számu*. Kerületi Könyvtar Gyermekrészlegének Olvasói, p. 172-94. Budapest, 1973.
What do children read and what did they read in 1936 and 1969 in the city branch library of the Ervin Szabo Municipal Library?

BALOGH, Ferencné. *Fiatal Olvasók a Tanácsi Könyvtárakban/ Tapasztalatok és Módszerek*. Közreadja az Eötvös Károly Megyei Könyvtár, Veszprém. Veszprém, 1974.
Young readers in the council libraries.

BAMBERGER, Richard. *Promoting the Reading Habit*. Paris, Unesco, 1975. (Reports and Papers on Mass Communication, No. 72.)
Includes chapters on reading activities in many countries, results of research on motivation, factors which influence reading interests, and methods for determining individual reading interests.

BATARI, Gyula. Az Irók és az Olvasás. *Könyvtáros*, Vol. 24, 7 S2, 1974, p. 420–1.
The writers and reading—an investigation by questionnaires carried out among 200 Hungarian writers and poets concerning their reading.

BISMARCK, Klaus von; GOTO, Kazuhiko; HAARMANN, Reinhard; MATHEWS, Virginia. *Die Rolle des Buches im Audiovisuellen Zeitalter*. Cologne, Westdeutscher Rund Funk, 1974.
A comparison of the role of the book in an audio-visual age in countries with social and cultural settings: the Federal Republic of Germany, Japan, the German Democratic Republic and the United States of America.

CHIU, Lian-Hwong. Reading Preferences of Fourth Grade Children Related to Sex and Reading Ability. *Journal of Educational Research*, Vol. 66, 1973, p. 369–73.
Investigation of United States children's reading preferences in relation to their sex and reading ability. Results indicated (a) boys preferred to read in the areas of biography, science, social studies and sports, while girls preferred adventure, fantasy, humour, and poetry; (b) there were no differences in reading preferences among high, average, and low level reading-ability groups.

DALE, Johs. A. *Litteratur og Lesing Omkring 1890*. Oslo, Det Norske Samlaget, 1974.

GEREBEN, Ferenc. *A Munkásság Olvasáskulturája—Kulturszociológai es Statisztikai Adatok Tükrében*. *A Könyv*, Vol. 9, 2 S2, 1974, p. 42–8.
Workers' reading culture as reflected in the data of cultural sociology and statistics.

GÖPFERT, Herbert; MEYER, Ruth; MUTH, Ludwig; RÜEGG, Walter. *Lesen und Leben*. Frankfurt-am-Main, Buchhändler-Vereinigung, Gmbh., 1975.
Issued in celebration of the German Booksellers Association's 150th anniversary of its founding, this collection is an interdisciplinary examination of the world of books and readers.
Section one is made up of research reports and analyses: Wolfgang R. Langenbucher, 'Die Demokratisierund des Lesens in der zweiten Leserevolution'; Rolf Eckmiller, Niels Galley, Otto-Joachim Grüsser, 'Neurobiologische und Nachrichtentechnische Grundlagen des Lesens';

Appendixes

Norbert Groeben, Brigitte Scheele, 'Zur Psychologie des Nicht-Lesens'; Wilhelm Salber, Linde Salber, 'Motivationen des Lesens and Nicht (-mehr)-Lesens'; Klaus Kippert, Christiane Geisthardt, 'Kritische Analyse der Leseerziehung in der Gegenwärtigen Gesellschaft'; Walter Rüegg, 'Lesen als Bedingung Humaner Existenz in einer Offenen Gesellschaft'; Ruth Meyer, 'Lesen als Mittel der Welterfahrung?'; Ulrich Saxer, 'Das Buch in der Medienkonkurrenz'.

The second section includes broad discussion: Christa Meves, 'Lesen und Familie'; Arnold Gromminger, 'Lesen und Schule'; Frolinde Balser, 'Lesen und Erwachsenenbildung'; Heinz Steinberg, 'Lesen in Öffentlichen Bibliotheken'; Peter Hartling, 'Der Autor—Kein Berufsbild'; Heinz Friedrich, 'Wer Druckt was für Wen and Warum?'; Peter Meuer, 'Aufgaben des Sortimentsbuchhandels in Unserer und Künftiger Zeit'; Wolfgang Strauss, 'Buchwissenschaft als Gemeinschaftsaufgabe des Buchhandels'; Ludwig Muth, 'Ausblicke'; Eymar Fertig, Heinz Steinberg, 'Literatur zur Lesenforschung'.

HANSEN, I. V. *Young People Reading: The Novel in Secondary Schools.* Second Century in Australian Education Series, No. 8. Melbourne, Melbourne University Press, 1973.

The author addresses teachers, parents, and young readers on the importance of reading fiction for young people. The first chapter, 'Young People Reading', discusses the development of children's literature since the eighteenth century. 'The Novel in the Conservative Classroom' argues for the inclusion of contemporary as well as classical literature in the curriculum, in order to provide a comprehensive view of literature. 'Why Read Novels Anyway?' asserts that the recognition of the human condition through the novel is a legitimate aim for any English programme for young people. The interpretive process is also discussed. 'Exploring through Fiction' includes reviews of six books, two appropriate for each of three age groups. 'The Wide Reading Scheme' discusses the recent assumption by reading of the dominant role in the English curriculum. 'A Micro-Sample: The Reading of Some Fifteen-Year-Olds' reviews a reading programme previously used by the author in his classes. The last chapter is a summary of the book. The appendixes contain lists of suggested and award-winning books.

HAVILAND, Virginia. Children: Their Reading Interests and Needs. *Children and Literature, Views and Reviews.* Glenview, Scott Foresman, 1973, Chapter 3.

Appendixes

Chapter 3 includes reprints of five articles that deal with such controversies as whether books should promote a certain value and whether children should be free to choose their own reading materials.

HOSODA, Hiroyuki. Reading Advisers at Bookshops. *Library Magazine*, No. 4, 1974.

HOUSEMAN, Ann Lord. Tuned in to the Entire Family—a Book Festival. *The Reading Teacher*, Vol. 27, December 1973, p. 246–8. Presents a school survey of favourite children's books and discusses family involvement in developing reading habits in elementary school students.

ISHIKAWA, Hiroyoshi. Concerning Readership Theory. *Studies on Editology*, No. 4, December 1973.

JAPAN COUNCIL FOR PROMOTION OF BOOK READING. *Memorandum on Motivating Book Reading*. Tokyo, Japan Council for Promotion of Book Reading, 1973.

JAPAN LIBRARIES ASSOCIATION. *White Paper on Library 1974*. Tokyo, Japan Libraries Association, 1974.

KAKINUMA, Takashi. Reading Promotion during World War II. *Library Magazine*, No. 3, 1974.

KAMARÁS, István. A Könyv és az Olvasás a Szovjet Kisvárosok Életében, *Könyvtári Figyeló*, Vol. 20, 3 S2, 1974, p. 259–67.

KANOSAWA, Seisuke. Promotion of Reading and Proper Reading Matter. *Journal of Japan Institute of Editology*, No. 14, July 1973.

KÁROLYI, Ágnes. *Kutatási Jelentés a Pedagógusok Olvasási Kulturájával Kapcsolatos Felmérésröl. Könyvtártudományi és Módszertani Központ, Országos Pedagógiai Könyvtár es Muzeum*, p. 98. Budapest, Nepmuv Prop. Iroda, 1974. (Summary in English.) Report on a survey conducted in connection with the reading culture of pedagogues.

KAWANAKA, Yasuhiro. Readers in the Age of Information. *Studies on Editology*, No. 4, December 1973.

Appendixes

KIDA, Junichiro. *Books, Information, Reading—Techniques of Their Utilization.* Tokyo, Publication News Company, 1973.

KIDA, Junichiro. *Reading Techniques of Contemporaries.* Tokyo, The Mainichi Newspapers, 1973.

KIKUCHI, Katsuhiro. Reading and the Organization of Readers. *Studies on Editology.* No. 4, December 1973.

KIRSCH, Dorothy Italie. *Current Expressed Reading Interests of Young Children.* Ed.D. dissertation, Hofstra University, New York, N.Y., 1973.
The purposes of this study were to survey expressed reading interests of first- and second-grade children from different geographic areas of the United States, with differing racial, ethnic, and socio-economic backgrounds; to compare expressed reading interests of children in grades 1 and 2 in an attempt to determine if interests change; and to probe the derivation of children's reading interests. The subjects were 1,078 first and second graders who were asked on a one-to-one basis to outline what they would like to read or have read to them. A structured interview followed. Responses were arranged into topics and classified in seven prearranged categories: information scientific, information historic, information 1970s, realistic fiction, imaginative fiction, humour, and poetry. The results indicated that significant differences in expressed reading interests were found in reference to sex, intelligence quotient, and reading level; girls showed greater interest in realistic fiction and less in information 1970s than boys; sex and racial ethnic group appeared to affect reading interest significantly for second graders; and significant differences in reading interests apparently existed between first- and second-grade children.

KOBAYASHI, Hiroshi. Libraries versus Readers. *Studies on Editology*, No. 4, December 1973.

KOBAYASHI, Kosuke. The Right to Read. *Studies on Editology*, No. 4, December 1973.

MACHILL, Horst (ed.). Der Buchhandel in Soziologischer Sicht. *Buch und Buchhandel in Zahlen, 1974.* Frankfurt-am-Main, Börsenverein des Deutschen Buchhandels, 1974.
A sociological study of the book trade.

MAEDA, Ai. *The Rise of Modern Readers*. Tokyo, Yuseido Co., 1973.

MAINICHI NEWSPAPERS. *Public Opinion Research on Reading, 1973*. Tokyo, The Mainichi Newspapers, 1973.

MAINICHI NEWSPAPERS. *Public Opinion Research on Reading, 1974*. Tokyo, The Mainichi Newspapers, 1974.

MANN, Margaret. *The Role of Books in Higher Education: A Selected Annotated Bibliography*. Sheffield, University of Sheffield, 1974.

MANN, Peter H. *Students and Books*. London and Boston, Routledge & Kegan Paul, Ltd, 1974.

MARTENS, Alexander U. *Mitmachen & Gewinnen*. Frankfurt-am-Main, Börsenverein des Deutschen Buchhandels, 1974.
A pamphlet about the sixteenth oral reading competition held in the Federal Republic of Germany, with broad support from government, by the German book trade.

MARTINEZ, Eugenia. Inchieste Sulle Letture dei Ragazzi. *Giornale della Libreria*. May 1975, p. 53–64.

MILLS & BOON. *The Facts about Romantic Fiction*. London, Mills & Boon, 1974.

MUNETAKE, Asako. Group Reading and the Participants. *Studies on Editology*, No. 4, December, 1973.

NATIONAL BOOK LEAGUE. *Books and Students*. London, The National Book League. 1974.

NORENG, Øystein. *Lesere og Lesing. Den Norske Bokklubbens Lesersosiologiske Undersøkelse*. Stabekk by Oslo, Den Norske Bokklubben, 1974.

NORENG, Øystein. *Lesing og Kommunikasjon. Kort Rapport*. Stabekk by Oslo, Den Norske Bokklubben, 1974.

NOSE, Hitoshi. On Readers. *Journal of Japan Institute of Editology*, No. 15, September 1973.

OGAMI, Sadao. *Reading Therapy—Its Theory and Practice*. Tokyo, Bunkyo Shoin Co., 1973.

OKUBO, Hisao. Literature about Readers. *Studies on Editology*, No. 4, December 1973.

PROGRESS PUBLISHERS. *Books in the Service of Peace, Humanism and Progress*. Moscow, Progress Publishers, 1974.
Proceedings of a Unesco-sponsored international symposium 12–15 September 1972, in celebration of International Book Year. (Available in Russian and English editions.)

ROBINSON, H. M.; WEINTRAUB, S. Research Related to Children's Interests and to Developmental Values of Reading. *Library Trends*, Vol. 22, 1973, p. 81–108.
Reviews techniques used and results of studies which concern themselves with the preferences of children to and for reading.
　　Discusses the fact that most studies do not deal with 'the disposition which impels an individual to seek opportunities and sources to read'.
　　The second part of the paper deals with studies that are related to the effects of reading, i.e. what values does the child obtain through reading. It is quite difficult to secure the students' perceptions of the value(s) in a selection.

ROWELL, C. Glennon. An Investigation of Factors Related to Change in Attitude toward Reading. *Journal of Reading Behavior*, Vol. 5, No. 4, autumn 1972–73, p. 266–72.
Studies the relationship between change in attitude towards reading and achievement in word identification, vocabulary and reading comprehension skills; sex; socio-economic status; and age. Seventy pupils in grades 4 through 8 were used. Statistically significant relationships were found between change of attitude towards reading and achievement in recognition of words in isolation, level of comprehension, recognition of letter sounds, and syllabication. No significant relationships were found between change in attitude toward reading and sex, socio-economic status, or age of the students.

SANTA, Eduardo. *El Libro en Colombia*. Bogotá, Instituto Colombiano de Cultura, 1973.

SANTA, Eduardo. *El Mundo Mágica del Libro*. Bogotá, Instituto Caro y Cuervo, 1974.

SATO, Tomonori. Bookshops as Information Depots. *Journal of Japan Institute of Editology*, No. 19, September 1974.

SCHEI, Per. *Litteratur over Landegrensene*. Bergen, Norges Handelshøyskole, 1973.

SCHMIDTCHEN, Gerhard. Lesekultur in Deutschland 1974. *Archiv für Soziologie und Wirtschaftsfragen des Buchhandels*, Vol. XXX.
Sociological analysis of the market for books for the German Publishers' Association.

SENUMA, Shigeki. Types of Readers in the Early Meiji Period. *Studies on Editology*, No. 4, December 1973.

SHIMIZU, Ikutaro. *How to Read Books*. Tokyo, Kodansha Ltd, 1973.

SHIMONAKA, Kunihiko *et al.* Round Table on Promotion of Book Reading in Future. *Journal of Japan Institute of Editology*, No. 19, 1973.

SMITH, Cari. B.; FAY, Leo. *Getting People to Read: Volunteer Programs That Work*. New York, N.Y., Delacorte Press, 1973. Paperback edition issued by Dell Press.
Descriptions of activities for the promotion of reading: (a) supportive, working within the schools; (b) supplemental, co-operating, but coming from outside schools; and (c) parallel, alternative programmes outside the schools.

SZABADI. Ilona. Az Olvasóvá Nevelés Clözményei az Óvodában. *Pedagógiai Szemle*, Vol. 24, SZ, 1974, p. 625–38.
The kindergarten preliminaries of educating children to become book lovers. Methods and results of an experiment carried out in the National Pedagogical Institute in 1965.

TORIKOSHI, Shin. *How to Choose the Right Books for Children*. Tokyo, Sanseido Co., 1973.

UNESCO. *Anatomy of an International Year. International Book Year, 1972*. Paris, Unesco, 1974. (Reports and Papers on Mass Communication, No. 71.)
A description, analysis and appraisal of International Book Year, 1972, by the Unesco Secretariat. This most successful celebration is seen as having far-reaching influence in many areas of the world.

YAMAMOTO, Taketoshi. Advertising of Publications and Purchasing Behavior of the Public. *Studies on Editology*, No. 4, December 1973.

Appendixes

ITEMS PUBLISHED IN 1975–76

AARON, R. L.; MILLER, L.; SMITH, E. Reading Habits of Behaviorally Disordered Males: A Study. *Journal of Reading*, Vol. 19, No. 1, 1975, p. 28–32.

This study sought to evaluate some aspects of the reading interests and tastes of a group of delinquent males between the ages of 13 and 19. Interviews were undertaken to define the extent of book completion for this population. Out of the interviews came the following information: (a) the relationship between method of book selection and percentage of books read; (b) the relationship between books selected and books completed; (c) the most popular titles.

ALEXANDER, J. E.; FILLER, R. C. Measures of Reading Attitudes. *Elementary English*, Vol. 52, No. 3, 1975, p. 376–8.

This article reviews eight scales which measure reading attitudes. The scales range from use with third graders to twelfth graders. Some are for use with good readers and some are for use with disabled readers. Though information on reliability and validity is given, there is no information given on the usefulness of the scale or the ease of administration. Complete references are given on where the reader can obtain the scale or more information about it.

ANKUDOWICZ, Janusz. *The Book in the Process of the Popularization of Science. Reading Research in Socialist Countries. Abridged Papers and Minutes of the Conference. Budapest, 15–18 October 1974.* Budapest, 1975, p. 143–7.

The popularization of both knowledge and science is an extensive social task and perspective. The phenomena and facts corroborating the justification of popular science books and non-fiction are discussed.

According to surveys conducted in Poland a few years ago, 13 per cent of city dwellers and 4 per cent of villagers read scientific and popular books. Today, however, the proportion of young readers in villages is already 17 per cent. The educational level of those who read non-fiction is four times higher than that of readers of fiction.

ASBJØRNSEN, Bjørn. De Norske Bokrevolusjoner. Fra Mørketid til Paperbacks og Bokklubber, Kristen Andersen, etc. *Tanke og Tone. Til Knut Tvedt.* Oslo, H. Aschehoug & Co. (W. Nygaard), 1976.

BAMBERGER, Richard. *Promoting the Reading Habit.* Paris, Unesco, 1975. (Reports and Papers on Mass Communication, No. 72.)

Appendixes

As a response to the close of the 1972 International Book Year sponsored by Unesco, this study was suggested concerning the reading habits of people throughout the world. A concern was expressed that without reading practice, reading skills already learned would be quickly lost and lifelong education would not take place. The author surveyed studies of reading habits throughout the world, noting differences in the readership of various countries and between adults and children. In almost every country usually twice as many children read as do adults, a difference that is even greater if one considers the difference between the life spans of each group. Topics explored in this study which are related to promoting reading habits are: the effective teaching of reading, the results of research on motivations for reading and reading interests, the factors which influence reading interests, the methods for determining individual reading interests, the promotion of developing reading interests and the reading habit, and some suggested tasks for research. Ideas are drawn from research performed in many countries. A bibliography is included.

Beliebte Fachzeitschriften. *Boersenblatt,* Vol. LXVI, August 1976, p. 1216–17.
Presents the results of a readership questionnaire and career data for individuals who have purchased a book during the past year.

BERG, Leila. *Reading and Loving.* London, Routledge & Kegan Paul, 1976.
Traces the varied ways babies learn to communicate and discusses the place of books in the lives of different groups in the community.

BJØRNSEN, Bjørn. *Hyorfor Leser Folk Ukeblad. Sammendrag av Odd Nordlands Bok: Ukeblad og Samfunn.* Oslo, Ukepressens Informasjonskontor, 1974.

BOGUE, Carole Jo Hoffman. *The Effect of a Token System on Reading Achievement and Attitude Toward Reading.* Ph.D. dissertation, University of Colorado, Boulder, 1975.
This study was designed to ascertain whether reading achievement and attitude towards reading of students in grades 2, 4, and 6 can be improved through implementation of a token system within regular reading programmes. Two schools were assigned to the experimental and two to the control treatment, with an equal number of classrooms from the three grades in each treatment group. All subjects

(Anglo- and Mexican-American students of lower-middle and lower socio-economic levels) were pre-tested in speed and accuracy, vocabulary, comprehension, and attitude toward reading. A reward system of tokens redeemable for reinforcing events was implemented in the reading programmes of the experimental groups. The control group received conventional reading instruction without the token system. Analysis of post-tests on reading achievement and attitude toward reading showed that the token system was effective for all indexes of reading achievement but not for reading attitude.

BOWERMASTER, Janet Marie. *The Effects of Choice on Children's Reading Comprehension and Attitudes*. M.S. Ed. thesis, University of Illinois, Urbana-Champaign, 1976.
This study was designed to test the effects of choice on the reading comprehension of ninety-two fifth- and sixth-grade students. Conducted in an elementary class-room, the test involved having each student read five passages and answer an interest questionnaire about the passages. The experimental variable in this study was choice of topics on a reading task. Children were assigned to either a cued-choice, blind-choice, or no-choice condition. In the cued-choice condition, children chose their reading topics from among alternatives which were clearly labelled. The blind-choice condition offered them a choice, but from among alternatives that were in blank folders so that they had no information about the alternatives. The no-choice condition assigned the selections to be read on a random basis. The analysis of central interest in this study was a sex by condition analysis of variance. The performance means were fairly low overall and were similar in magnitude for both sexes. However, the boys in the cued-choice condition performed substantially better than the boys in the blind-choice and no-choice conditions. The girls had no apparent pattern which could be related to the manipulation of the choice variable.

BROWN, Eleanor Drum. *The Role of the English Teacher in Encouraging Recreational Reading*. Ed.D. dissertation, State University of New York, Albany, 1975.
This study describes the role of the ninth grade English teacher and the use of class-room resources in promoting recreational reading. The range of recreational reading and the reading interests of 2,255 ninth grade pupils in nine high schools near Albany, New York, were identified, and the factors which appear to be associated

with pupils' recreational reading were inferred. Thirty-four ninth grade English teachers participated in structured interviews and responded to a questionnaire. A jury of experts on literature for young adults and on methods of teaching English teachers rated the teachers on their encouragement of recreational reading. A major finding of the study was that elements of pupil background (sex and father's education and occupation) appear to exert more influence on pupil interest in reading than does the teacher. When the interest in reading does exist, however, the teacher does promote increased recreational reading. Other findings were that recreational reading ranks last among leisure time pursuits for boys and next to last for girls and that the books which pupils read for class did not make them want to read more of the same kind of book for pleasure.

CERDA, Hugo. *Literatura Infantil y Clases Sociales.* Bogotá, 1975.

CERLAL. *Seminario sobre los Hábitos, Niveles a Intereses de Lectura.* Bogotá, 1975.

CHILD STUDY ASSOCIATION OF AMERICA. WEL-MET, NEW YORK. *Children's Books of the Year 1974.* 50 Madison Avenue, New York, N.Y. 10010, Child Study Press, 1975.
The books in this annual listing have been reviewed and selected by the Children's Book Committee, a voluntary group of parents, teachers, librarians, writers and specialists in various related fields. The listing contains books written for the nursery years through age 13. Titles are arranged, for the most part, according to age groups and are further differentiated into topical divisions which are reflective of the interests and abilities of children. Non-fiction books of information are listed in topical groupings under a special interest heading. Other sections include collections, poetry, holidays, books for parents and children, reprints and new editions, and paperback reprints. Each listing contains bibliographic information, a brief annotation of the book, and the suggested age level. Starred titles indicate books considered by the committee to be of outstanding merit.

CRAMER, Eugene Hartley. *A Study of the Relationships Among Mental Imagery, Reading Comprehension, and Reading Attitude of Eleventh and Twelfth Grade Students.* Ph.D. dissertation, University of Wisconsin, Madison, 1975.
The purpose of this study was to investigate relationships among three concepts associated with reading; ability to comprehend printed

prose, vividness of self-reported mental imagery, and attitude toward reading. Data showed no significant relationship between mental imagery and reading comprehension, a relatively low but significant correlation between reading attitude and mental imagery, a significant correlation between reading comprehension and reading attitude, and high attitude toward reading as a function of a combination of high imagery and high comprehension.

DEMPSEY, Jane. *Diagnosis and Prescriptive Strategies Designed to Bring Back the Joy.* Paper presented at the Annual Meeting of the California Reading Association Conference, Fresno, Calif., November 1975.

The diagnostic and prescriptive strategies presented in this paper are based on the assumption that reading is language, reading is understanding, reading is not an exact process, reading is responding, and reading is enjoyable. The diagnostic information needed includes basic skills as well as attitudes towards reading and reading interests. Sources for obtaining this information include a variety of group methods such as administering standardized intelligence and achievement tests, and individual procedures such as administering a miscue analysis inventory and holding individual conferences. Prescriptive strategies for bringing the joy of reading to students include making a wide variety of books available for student selection and scheduling a reading time in addition to skill instruction time.

DONELSON, Kenneth. *Books for You.* A book-list prepared by the Committee on the Senior High School Booklist of the National Council of Teachers of English. Champaign, Ill., National Council of Teachers of English, 1976.

A book-length list of reading for students in senior high school organized by topic, and including both fiction and non-fiction in each of over forty sections.

DRESSLER, Irmgard. *Pupils as Library Users.* Results of an investigation among pupils attending the 5th to 10th forms in the German Democratic Republic. Reading research in socialist countries. Abridged papers and minutes of the conference, Budapest, 15–18 October 1974. Budapest, 1975, p. 45–51.

In 1972, a major investigation of library use among pupils attending the 5th to 10th forms was conducted in the German Democratic Republic. The children had to complete a questionnaire. The investigation took place in ten children's and ten adult libraries in regional towns of different size. Answers were requested to the following questions: 'What kind of books do children select for their school work and what for their individual interests? What kind of relationship can be established between the children's choice and the guidance provided by the librarian?' The total number of the fully completed questionnaires was 1,769.

The present investigation has confirmed the fact that a better familiarity with the library results in a more extensive use. Further on, the necessity of the systematical introduction to the use of the adult library is proved, too. The bases for a child to become a regular reader must be laid in early childhood. A close co-operation among all the participants in the education of youth is necessary to enable pupils to make proper use of libraries and books.

FAKTA A/S. *Undersøkelse Vedrørende Ukebladlesning Blant Butikk-personale, Januar–Desember 1972.* Oslo, Fakta A/S, Institutt for Markedsføring, Samfunnsanalyser, Socialforskning, 1974.

FAULSTICH, Werner. Literaturwissenschafter und Buecher. *Archiv fuer Sociologie und Wirtschaftsfragen des Buchhandels*, Vol. XXXVII, p. 320–6.
Presents the results of a study of the recreation, reading preferences and habits of literary specialists, as well as the sources from which they derive information for book purchases.

FOGARASSY, Miklós; KAMARÁS, István. Egy Nemzetközi Olvasásszocio-lógiai Befogadás-vizsgálat Módszertani Tanulságai, p. 492–508. *Könyvtári Figyelö*, No. 5, 1975.
Methodological results of an international reading—sociological reception-investigation.
In 1974, on the initiative and under the leadership of the Centre for Library Science and Methodology, Budapest, in co-operation with the methodological departments of national libraries in Moscow, Sofia and Warsaw, an international comparative investigation started in the field of reading sociology. The reception of three Hungarian short stories was the subject of this investigation. The experimentees reading the short stories were chosen from among persons, using libraries. The first group consisted of 40–50 year-old iron-masters, the second group of 40–50 year-old skilled women workers from the textile industry, the third one of 17-year-old secondary school pupils and the fourth group included librarians.

The first part of this study, 'From the Assumption to the Questionnaire' published in two parts, presents the research plan, its assumptions, the short stories and the questionnaire applied for the research. It deals with the opinion of experts in literature, aesthetics, psychology and sociology about the research plan. The second part of the study 'Measuring the Reception and Interpretation of the Literary Work' deals with the methodological problems arising in the course of data processing: with the measuring of likes or dislikes, with the judgement of literary values as well as with the four kinds of methods in the course of measuring the interpretation of the literary work.

HEATHINGTON, Betty Sue. *The Development of Scales to Measure Attitudes toward Reading*. Ed.D. dissertation, University of Tennessee, 1975.
The purpose of this study was to develop an instrument or instruments to measure the attitudes towards reading of children in grades 1 to 6. The Likert-type scale was chosen as the most appropriate type of instrument to meet established criteria. Two rural schools and two urban schools with normally distributed populations according to ability and socio-economic levels were used in the study.

HIPPLE, Theodore W. *et al*. The Novels Adolescents Are Reading. *Research Bulletin*, Florida, Educational Research and Development Council, Vol. X, No. 1, Autumn 1975.
This monograph reports the results of a national study conducted to determine the names of the novels students are most commonly required to read in their high school English courses and the names of their favourite novels, and to recommend methods for teaching novels. The sample for the survey was drawn from the membership of the Conference of Secondary School English Department Chairmen, an affiliate of the National Council of Teachers of English. The research instrument used was a questionnaire. An extensive narrative summary of results is provided along with a brief bibliography of books and articles about the teaching of novels.

INTERNATIONAL READING ASSOCIATION. The Visible Word. An Essay on the Occasion of the Bicentennial of the United States of America. *The Reading Teacher*, Vol. XXIX, January 1976, p. 325-31.

JOHNS, J. L. Reading Preferences of Urban Students in Grades Four through Six. *Journal of Educational Research*, Vol. 68, No. 8, 1975, p. 306–9.

This study investigated the preferences of 597 fourth, fifth and sixth grade pupils for illustrations, settings and characters similar to and different from their own environment. A questionnaire was prepared with fifteen found choices, all taken from modern realistic fiction books for children. Significant (.001) preferences were expressed for stories or books depicting middle-class settings, characters with positive self-concepts, and characters in positive group interactions. The results did not support a need for reading materials attuned to real-life experiences of upper-grade urban students.

JOHNSON, Connie. *100 Activities to Motivate Primary Reading.* Minneapolis, Minn., T. S. Denison & Company, Inc. (5100 West 82nd Street, Minneapolis, Minn. 55437.)

In this teaching guide 100 reading activities are suggested to provide ways for children to use their reading skills for enjoyment and to motivate independent reading. Activities are grouped into suggestions for individuals, small groups and entire classes. Some topics for individual activities are book buttons, taped reading, a book bank, a giant book, riddles and a personal diary. Some suggested small group activities are unison reading, story comics, puppet plays, book parades, quiet hideaways and skill games. Some ideas for whole class activities are mood reading, ethnic book displays, multisensory reading, candid camera, a book surprise corner and a poetry day.

KATSÁNYI, Sándor. *Historical Culture—Historical Reading Material —Reading Research in Socialist Countries. Abridged Papers and Minutes of a Conference. Budapest, 15–18 October 1974.* Edited by National Széchényi Library Centre for Library Science and Methodology. Budapest, 1975, p. 135–42.

In 1976, the Hungarian Council of Ministers declared that 'pedagogical research serving the development of public education' is a main trend of national research. The aim of the research is to throw light on the question of how school education and extracurricular education can be connected in a way that may serve in the future as a basis for permanent education.

After the completion of the plan of research, in October 1973, questionnaire interviews were made with 1,200 persons. Their distribution was the following: 400 industrial apprentices and

400 young skilled workmen. In the control groups there were: 100 grammar-school pupils, 100 administrators and 100 aged skilled workmen.

Permanent culture and reading had to be investigated in the direction of historical cultural change after school-leaving. Here the skilled workers, age group, 40–60, had the highest correct recognition of historical personalities. The assumption that the social environment (including the influence of the mass media, too) exerts a strong influence on the development of the knowledge of facts already in the school years seems well grounded.

It can be stated that reading plays a special role in the permanent acquisition of knowledge after school-leaving. While in the case of age groups that left school the degree of efficiency of cultural impulses influencing them generally decreases from factual knowledge to abstraction, a precisely opposite trend is observable among readers.

LAMME, L. L. Are Reading Habits and Abilities Related? *Reading Teacher*, Vol. 30, No. 1, 1976, p. 21–7.
This study sought to answer a number of questions about the relationship between children's reading habits and their reading abilities. The subject for this study was the fourth grade population of an elementary school. The students' reading habits and abilities were followed for a three-year period. Conclusions indicate the following: (a) the reading habit which is most consistently sensitive to reading ability measures is the habit of seeking out books by known authors; (b) the assumption that children's reading habits bear a strong relationship to their reading abilities was not confirmed; and (c) reading habits are highly individualistic.

LATHAM, William (ed.). *The Road to Effective Reading. Proceedings of the Annual Study Meeting of the United Kingdom Reading Association*. London, Ward Lock Educational.
Papers presented at the tenth annual study conference of the United Kingdom Reading Association, held at Totley-Thornbridge College of Education, Sheffield, are included in this report. The conference theme centred on the proposition that learning to read is a long-term developmental process beginning in pre-school life and language experience and reaching fruition in the study skills of the effective adult reader. Topics for papers include: early language development, reading readiness, beginning reading, the reading curriculum for the middle years of schooling, reading comprehension factors, teacher

education, silent reading, listening skills, study skills, reading habits and interests of adults, reading achievement, and the Right To Read Program in the United States of America.

McLaughlin, J.; Andrews, J. The Reading Habits of Deaf Adults in Baltimore. *American Annals of the Deaf*, Vol. 120, No. 5, 1975, p. 497–501.
A representative sample of thirty-six urban deaf adults were interviewed to discover the extent and nature of the reading material they enjoyed. This paper presents the analysis of the interviews. The significant findings are: (a) those interviewed read principally the daily newspaper and magazines; (b) books were read less frequently than magazines and newspapers; (c) individuals over 50 years of age read more than those under 50; (d) the adults who used manual communication read more than adults who used only oral communication. Implications for the teacher of reading to the deaf are presented.

Manitoba Department of Education, Winnipeg, Canada. *A Banquet of Books. An Assortment of Engrossing Books for All Ages and Reading Levels*, September 1975.
The books listed in this annotated bibliography have been selected to assist teachers, librarians and other interested persons in choosing books for reluctant readers. The books present a wide range of high interest material which is not always at a low reading level. Books are listed in three categories: picture books, intended mostly for use with primary grade children; fiction—adventure and mustery, animal stories, fantasy and science fiction, sports stories, miscellaneous fiction and story collections; and non-fiction—biography, haunted houses, monsters and unidentified flying objects, hobbies and crafts, the world of entertainment, Indians of North America, science, sports, wild animals and pets, wings and wheels, and the world at war. Annotations for each entry include bibliographic data, a brief description, print size, vocabulary range, and reading and interest levels.

Maruniak, Peter *et al. Some Results of the Research into Reader Needs in Slovakia. On the Basis of the Investigations Carried out in the Village Krivà. Reading Research in Socialist Countries. Abridged Papers and Minutes of the Conference, Budapest, 15–18 October 1974.* Budapest, 1975, p. 123–9.
The surveys were taken in the village Krivà in 1961–62 and in 1970. These investigations carried out in the same decade, made comparisons possible.

Appendixes

The village Krivà has an agricultural character even though the majority of the population works in different branches of economy. Cultural and social life is limited, and the public library is the only institution provided with funds; besides the public library there are some further libraries in the village. The investigation proved that youth under 15 constituted the most significant group of readers.

Both surveys were directed at private libraries which had become significant sources of literature. In 1962 there was not a single family which bought sixteen to twenty books while in 1969 there were three such families. The increased interest in books is expressed by the summarized amounts spent on books by households.

The survey in 1970 showed also that the number of books read grew in proportion to the level of education. The majority of respondents said that reading was primarily recreation for them. The next group wanted to acquire new knowledge, emotional experiences; educative examples were also given as reason.

The repeated investigation in 1970 showed that readers' interest had improved for the past ten years but, on the other hand, literary taste was not yet satisfactory. There is still a lot to do in the field of the readers' education.

MERRITT, John E. (ed.), *New Horizons in Reading. Proceedings of the International Reading Association World Congress on Reading.* Newark, Del., International Reading Association, 1976.

This volume contains a selection of the papers presented at the fifth International Reading Association World Congress on Reading. Part one, 'Reading: An Expanding Concept', contains papers that examine such topics as literal comprehension, miscue analysis, and children's literature and reading. Part two, 'Some Implications for the Reading Curriculum', contains papers on such topics as language and the reader, language games and literacy, reading to learn, evaluation of progress in spare-time reading, and sequence and structure in reading development. Part three, 'Writing Systems and Early Reading: Comparative Perspectives', contains papers that examine such topics as writing systems in Japan, the teaching of spelling, and some unexplained aspects of early reading. Part four, 'The Reader and the Media', contains papers on such topics as new developments on readability, content bias in adult reading materials, and reading and television in the United States. Part five, 'Special Problems', contains papers which discuss such topics as promoting reading habits, class size and reading development, and reading comprehension in fifteen countries. Part six, 'Raising Teaching Standards', contains papers on such topics as the rationale for competency-based in-service education, and evaluation and accountability.

MUTH, Ludwig. Zugaenge (und Hendernisse) Zum Fachbuch. *Archiv fuer Soziologie und Wirtschaftsfragen des Buchhandels*, Vol. XXXVII, p. 315–19.
Presents nine interferences with career-related reading; in schools, in the place of work, and in bookselling. Suggests three ways in which these problems can be met.

NATIONAL BOOK CENTRE OF BANGLADESH. Sample Survey of the Reading Habits of Metropolitan Children of Bangladesh. *Newsletter*, Regional Centre for Book Development in Asia, Karachi, Pakistan. Vol. XVII, No. 3, July 1976, p. 5–6.
Interviewed 388 pupils from 8 to 16 years of age in Docca city schools and ninety-six parents/guardians for relevant information. Findings summarized: (a) boys and girls are mainly interested in reading detective stories; 30.7 per cent female and 57.2 per cent male students usually read detective stories; (b) 49.7 per cent female and 65.3 per cent male students like to read short stories and juvenile fiction; (c) 44 per cent female and 48.7 per cent male students expressed interest in folk and fairy tales. Comparatively, science books were read mainly by male students (39.1 per cent), whereas only 14 per cent girl students read these books; (d) the children's page in daily newspapers had the highest number of readers among children and adolescents—54.3 per cent male students and 51.3 per cent female students; (e) 38.1 per cent male and 30.1 per cent female students state that they subscribe to periodicals; (f) of the total number of students interviewed, 30 per cent were regular readers and 6 per cent did not read at all; (g) boys and girls spend an average of one hour per day in reading books; 49.3 per cent of them buy books at sometime or another; (h) 78 per cent of the male and female students use school libraries and reading rooms while the remaining 22 per cent collect books through different sources; (i) 93.7 per cent parents/guardians encourage their children to read books other than textbooks; 59.4 per cent parents/guardians buy books for their children, spending an average of Tk.370.80 per year; (j) 81.2 per cent of the teachers persuade children to do general reading; (k) 82.3 per cent parents/guardians maintain that there is a shortage in the availability of readable books in the market, while 50 per cent state that the books available lack originality; (l) 53 per

cent parents/guardians expressed the opinion that reading habits had the highest influence on children, while 60 per cent believed that the influence of television has a higher rating.

NORDLAND, Odd. *Ukeblad og Samfunn. Funksjonsanalyse.* Oslo, Universitetsforlaget, 1973.

OJA, Kaljo. *The Social Role of the Library in Forming the Reader's Inquiries. Reading Research in the Socialist Countries. Abridged Papers and Minutes of a Conference. Budapest, 15–18 October 1974.* Edited by National Széchényi Library Centre for Library Science and Methodology. Budapest, 1975, p. 110–15.

Today's public library must be a leading institution of permanent education. As to the readers, they should have free choice of publications. The social function of the library is to find out the reader's real interests, his reading system and to plan the improvement of his reading.

In Estonia two studies were conducted in 1967 and in 1971–72. The first one gives a general basis for the characterization of the social role of Estonian public libraries, the second one embraces the problem in depth from the point of view of individual readers' advisory service.

RONEY, Richard Craig. *The Effects of Two Promotional Teaching Techniques on the Amount of Personal Reading and Selection of Books by Fourth Grade Children.* Ph.D. dissertation, University of Colorado, Boulder, 1975.

This study was designed to consider whether, by introducing fourth-grade children to books by two promotional techniques, teachers can influence: (a) the amount of personal reading done by children; (b) which books these children select for personal reading; and (c) the attitude of the children towards the books they select. In each of ten classes selected for the study, the teachers promoted equal numbers of books by reading segments of books to their children and by a bulletin board display. Other books designated control books were not promoted. All books were randomly selected and assigned to each of the three treatment groups for each class. The books ranged in difficulty from a readability of 2.5 to 5.5 and included a variety of fiction of interest to fourth-grade children. Each class received two paperback copies of all books in each of the three treatment groups. The children were permitted to borrow these books and read them at home or in class during free reading time. Results of this study indicated that the use of promotional techniques by teachers did not have a uniform effect on children. Where the techniques were effective, oral reading of segments of books was generally more effective than use of a bulletin board display.

SCHAEFER, Karl Friedrich. *Leseprobe. 1976–1*. Munich-Vienna, Franz Schneider Verlag, 1976.
A collection of excerpts for students, introducing them to twenty-five authors and eight illustrators and their books.

SCHAEFER, Karl Friedrich. *Leseprobe. 1976–2*. Munich-Vienna, Franz Schneider Verlag, 1976.
A second collection, including excerpts from the work of thirty-two authors and fifteen illustrators of juvenile books.

SCHOLTZ, Ann Judith. *An Investigation of the Role of Interest as a Factor in Reading Comprehension*. M.Ed. thesis, Rutgers, State University of New Jersey, 1976.
This study was an investigation into the relationships between reading interests and reading comprehension as demonstrated by a group of fifth graders who rated reading passages for interest and then were checked for comprehension of these same passages. A seven-point rating inventory, ranging from a 'liked very, very much' rating to a 'disliked very, very much' rating, was used to measure the reader's interest. The mean reading achievement grade-level score for the 110 fifth-grade students participating in this study was 5.9 at the time of the study's testing programme. It was concluded that expressed interest is not a factor which affects reading comprehension. Reading interest patterns do provide information as to what children will read, but are not significant in determining the level of reading comprehension.

SCHWARZNER, Brigitta. Motivation im Betrieb und Moeglichkeiten der Motivation Analyse. *Archiv fuer. Sociologie und Wirtschaftfragen des Buchhandels*, Vol. XXXVII, p. 373–423.
A very thorough study of the motivation of bookseller's clerks.

STELMAKH, V. D. *Study of the Reading of Belles-Lettres. Reading Research in Socialist Countries. Abridged Papers and Minutes of a Conference. Budapest, 15–18 October 1974*. Edited by National Széchényi Library Centre for Library Science and Methodology, Budapest, 1975, p. 181–5.

Appendixes

The study of the reading of *belles-lettres* is connected with the general interest shown in artistic reading matter. Mass interest in a certain work of art is determined by social influence. The spectator gets from the film to the work if the film is interesting but frequently the active rejection of the film is the motive force.

Another example of the factors influencing reading is the popularity of works published in a novel newspaper. It was Lenin's thought to publish cheap novels in the form of a proletarian newspaper for the people. According to the data received, the investigated persons read the book, because it was 'recommended by friends, acquaintances, colleagues'.

From the point of view of selecting the reading matter the genre-thematic characteristic of the work is the second most important motive for the readers.

Literary-artistic interest and artistic taste is the personal, individual characteristics of every person. But on the basis of the development of individual tastes the aesthetical tastes of society are accumulated. Each person's reading culture develops; at the same time the people's general artistic level arises and true aesthetic ideas and opinions get shaped.

SVENDSEN, Arnljot Strømme. Billigboken. Kristen Andersen, etc. *Tanke og Tone. Til Knut Tvedt.* Oslo, H. Aschehoug & Co. (W. Nygaard), 1976.

SWINGER, Alice Kruckeberg. *The Effects of a Long Term Literature Program on the Participating Grade Six Students and Their Teachers.* Ph.D. dissertation, Ohio State University, Columbus, 1975.
Eleven teachers participated in an in-service programme, read to their sixth-grade students, and allowed them silent reading time and follow-up activities for eight months. Treatment group boys demonstrated more positive attitudes on the concepts 'Acting Out Stories' and 'Talking About Books in School' than control group boys. Treatment group girls demonstrated significantly more positive attitudes on the concept 'Teacher Reading to Students' than control group girls. On a semantic differential scale students ranked reading-related topics most highly. Students' response to the concepts 'Writing in School', 'Acting Out Stories', and 'Making Objects Explain a Story' were mixed, although student journal entries expressed emotional involvement, interest and identification with characters.

Reading achievement levels in the treatment group were comparable to those in the control group, but the treatment group showed gains in literacy knowledge. Finally, the informal approach to the literature programme did not produce variation in literature appreciation, nor was any relationship between teachers' and students' attitudes discerned.

SZABADIDÖ ÉS MÜVELÖDÉS. Tanulmányok a Magyar Szabadiö Kutatások Köréböl. Fel. Szerk. Fukász György. Budapest, 1974. *Tudományos Ismeretterjesztö Társulat.* 360 p. (Leisure Time and Education. Studies on Leisure Time in Hungary.)

Nine studies included in this volume are arranged in two large groups, according to their topics: 'Leisure Time and Society' and 'Leisure Time-Education-recreation'. The studies are introduced by Zsuzsa Ferge's paper entitled: 'Contribution to the Investigation of Hungarian Time Balance'. The studies are followed by the bibliography of the related Hungarian literature covering the period 1961–73.

In the course of the currently conducted research—dealing with vocational students—considerable steps were taken that time balances should include also the description of the way of life. After having presented some analytical procedures, she summarizes her findings with the statement that time balance is a particularly useful tool in the research of society but we are still at the beginning to make the best of possibilities hidden in it.

SZENTIRMAI, Lázló. *Reading Habits of University Students as Revealed by a One-week Time Budget Survey. Reading Research in Socialist Countries. Abridged Papers and Minutes of a Conference. Budapest, 15–18 October 1974.* Edited by National Széchényi Library Centre for Library Science and Methodology. Budapest, 1975, p. 65–73.

In April 1973, an investigation was carried out among the students of the University of Szeged. Diaries of activities were filled by more than three hundred students. The aim of the investigation was to examine the content of the way of life of students with the help of the structure of activities, above all working and leisure activities with special regard to reading. The activities were divided into seven broad groups and sixty-five kinds of activities.

It became obvious that the reading of non-compulsory literature takes on the average 4.66 hours a week and within the leisure time this is the second most time-consuming pastime.

Appendixes

The examination proved that students of higher education belong entirely to the category of readers. It is interesting to find out that women read more than men. Students in the first year read less and with the progress of years the number of hours devoted to reading increases. The university library helps students with professional literature and that is what students read in the reading-room.

Reading is a leisure activity which is carried out regularly by every student with more or less frequency and for different lengths of time. Regularity means reading at least one book a month. The university library plays an essential role in the structure of activities of university students' way of life.

TIBBETS, S. L. Intelligence and Children's Reading Preferences. *California Journal of Educational Research*, Vol. 26, No. 2, 1975, p. 89–91.
A brief review of the research which relates a child's intellectual abilities and reading preferences. The conclusion of the review is that while differences in intelligence alone will not prevent children from developing similar reading interests, intelligence may be a factor in determining the range, amount and quality of a child's reading material.

TVETERÅS, Harald L. Studies of Readers and Readers' Interest in Norway. In: Foster E. Mohrhardt (ed.), *Reading in a Changing World*. Papers presented at the 38th session of the IFLA General Council. Budapest, 1977. Munich, Verlag Dokumentation, 1976. (IFLA Publications, 5.)

VARGA, Béla. A Munkásság Olvásáskulturája. Kérdöives Felmérés, 1975. 49 lev. 65 t. Kézirat. The workers' reading culture. Investigation in inquiry form. (Manuscript.)
Prior to Hungary's liberation, newspaper reading or at least the demand for it was a characteristic feature of the workers as well as the peasants of the society. Today the reading of daily papers is an essential necessity for the adult members of the society.

On the average every fourth person has subscribed to a newspaper or has purchased a daily paper regularly. In this county more than half of the workers habitually reads—besides a newspaper—some illustrated weekly magazine.

According to the experiences gained by the investigation the intensity of book reading depends on three determining factors:

school qualification, the occupied place in social division of labour, and the way of life, determined by dwelling place, since a large part of workers lives in villages and attends to work daily in the city.

According to the investigation more than half of the workers asked reads books regularly, others only occasionally and 2–3 per cent admittedly never.

The next comprehensive chapter of the accomplished investigation in county Veszprém in 1974 deals with the books borrowed by adults from the council public libraries. Here the questions deal with the quality of reading and in this field, no doubt, there are problems yet.

In the county more than 68 per cent of the workers read, first of all, the books from their own library. In county relations the trade-union libraries have the fewest readers, and utilization of council public libraries is much higher.

The investigation also proved that, in general, elementary school qualification is that turning-point which arouses the interest in a more regular completion and development of one's own library in an increased degree.

Finally, the investigation deals with the situation of public libraries in the county and with their role in the life of reading workers.

The manuscript is supplemented by sixty-five statistical tables of the investigation.

WEISS, Margit. *On the Activities of Central Libraries Working Within Village Associations. Reading Research in the Socialist Countries. Abridged Papers and Minutes of a Conference. Budapest, 15–18 October 1974.* Edited by National Széchényi Library, Centre for Library Science and Methodology. Budapest, 1975, p. 94–102.
In 1972 there were 8,777 towns and villages in the German Democratic Republic. Eighty-five per cent of them had less than 2,000 and 50 per cent less than 500 inhabitants. This was the reason that village associations were established. These associations represent the town and villages and are responsible for their social life. Within these village associations central libraries came into existence. They comprise averagely five to eight villages with 4,000–7,000 inhabitants.

The central libraries have, first of all, the task to meet the users' demand. A percentage of 55.8 expressed demands for literature with a view to education and continued education. The proportion of central library users who read for leisure time purposes was 98.6 per cent.

Appendixes

The interviews made it evident that further researches and surveys should be made more thoroughly to improve the work of libraries with their users in the future.

WILMOT, Margaret Price. *An Investigation of the Effect upon the Reading Performance and Attitude toward Reading of Elementary Grade Students, of Including in the Reading Program a Period of Sustained, Silent Reading.* Ph.D. dissertation, University of Colorado, Boulder, 1975.

An experiment was conducted with 576 students (in grades 2, 4, and 6) to determine if there were significant differences in reading performance and attitude towards reading between students in programmes which included a daily period of sustained, silent reading (SSR) and those in programmes which did not. The SSR involved students and teachers in daily silent reading of material of their own choice with no evaluation associated with the reading. Attitude towards reading was measured by the Wilmot Reading Attitude Inventory, reading performance by the vocabulary and comprehension subtests of the Gates Primary B and Survey D Reading Tests. Results of analysis showed that students in grades 4 and 6 in the SSR group had significantly better attitudes towards reading than those in control groups in those grades, control group student's performance on comprehension was significantly better in all grades, and there was no significant difference between the groups in performance on the vocabulary test.

WILSON, Roy Russell, Jr. *In-Depth Book Discussions of Selected Sixth Graders: Response to Literature.* Ph.D. dissertation, Ohio State University, Columbus, 1975.

The four major purposes of this study were: to examine and describe the in-depth discussions by selected sixth graders of specific books in an attempt to characterize the nature of the responses; to compare four strategies which were employed for initiating the different discussions; to discover the range of personal involvement which sixth graders may have in literature; and to examine one discussion leader's role. In this study, eight sixth-grade children were exposed to five books of different genres followed by a discussion of each book. Seven of the children heard the books read aloud to their class as a daily, continuing experience by the class-room teacher. The eighth child read the books to herself. Personal constructs and contrasts which had particular meaning to the individual were elicited. It was concluded from this study that children need to have frequent opportunity to discuss their reading in a meaningful way; in discussing books with children up to age 12, emphasis should be placed on the content and theme of a book rather than literary analysis; interest in reading appears to be self-generating; and children with little interest in books appear to gain more from in-depth discussions.

Appendix 2
Select bibliography
on reading motivation[1]

The items which follow were chosen from the collection of the Educational Resources Information Center (ERIC), an educational information network and programme of the Dissemination and Resources Division of the National Institute of Education, Department of Health, Education, and Welfare of the United States. The articles or monographs with an ED number are references which have been abstracted in Resources in Education *(RIE), a monthly journal. The entries followed by EJ numbers refer to journal articles cited in* The Current Index to Journals in Education.

While the journal articles must be procured from the original publisher, items marked ED can be obtained in either microfiche or paper copy from the ERIC Documentation Reproduction Service, P.O. Box 190, Arlington, VA 22210 (United States). Interested readers may also contact the information centres listed at the end of this bibliography, which maintain microfiche collections of ERIC documents.

Invaluable assistance in the compilation of this bibliography was received from Dr William Higgins and Ms Mary Campbell of the staff of the Educational Reference Center of the National Institute of Education and from Mr Robert Ellis of the staff of Time-Life Books, Inc.

ALILUNAS, Leo J. Children Read 'Bugs Bunny', 'Dear Abby' Too. *Quill and Scroll*, Vol. XLVIII, No. 4, April 1974, p. 18–19. (EJ 097 793.)

ALSOBROOKS, Jennye B. Motivated: They Will Read. Paper presented at the Language Arts and Reading Conference, Ball State University, 1970. (ED 045 310.)

1. Compiled by the Academy for Educational Development.

Appendixes

ANDERSON, C. Arnold *et al. Students, Teachers and Opportunity Perceptions in Kenya, 1961–68,* Vol. II. *Final Report.* Chicago, Ill., University of Chicago, 1969. (ED 040 636.)

ASHLEY, L. F. *Children's Reading and the 1970's.* Toronto, McClelland & Stewart Ltd, 1972. (ED 094 314.)

ASKOV, Eunice N.; FISCHBACH, Thomas J. An Investigation of Primary Pupils' Attitudes toward Reading. *Journal of Experimental Education,* Vol. XLI, No. 3, spring, 1973, p. 1–7. (EJ 082 199.)

BAMBERGER, Richard. Developing Lifelong Reading Interests and Reading Habits. *Bookbird,* Vol. X, No. 2, 1972, p. 28–31. (EJ 063 981.)

——. *Promoting the Reading Habit.* Paris, Unesco, 1975. (Reports and Papers on Mass Communication, No. 72.) (ED 112 370.)

BAZANY, M. The Work-Oriented Adult Literacy Pilot Project in Iran. *Literacy Work,* Vol. II, Nos. 1–2, July–September 1972, p. 1–69. (EJ 065 498.)

BETTS, Emmett Albert. Aerospace: Potent Motivation for Reading. *Education,* Vol. XCII, No. 4, April–May 1972. (EJ 059 528.)

BHOLA, H. S. Functional Literacy—the Concept and the Programme. Keynote address at the Thirteenth Annual Study Conference, University of East Africa, Nairobi, Kenya, 17–18 August 1969. (ED 038 566.)

BLAIR, Judith R. *The Status of Nonfiction in the Reading Interests of Second, Third, and Fourth Graders.* M.Ed. thesis, Rutgers University, State University of New Jersey, 1974. (ED 095 481.)

BRACKEN, Dorothy Kendall; MALMQUIST, Eve (eds.). *Improving Reading Ability Around the World. Proceedings of the Third International Reading Association World Congress on Reading, Sydney, Australia, August 7–9, 1970.* Newark, Del., International Reading Association, 1971. (ED 059 007.)

BRAINE, Lila Ghent. *Pattern Perception in Relation to Reading Habits, Final Report.* Washington, D.C., George Washington University, 1967. (ED 087 993.)

BRINK, R. E. M. VAN DEN. *Book Reading, Borrowing and Buying Habits. Report of the Eighteenth Congress, Amsterdam, the Netherlands, June 9–15, 1968.* Geneva, International Publishers Association, 1968. (ED 059 736.)

BROOKS, Ruth Ann. *An Investigation of the Relationship Between Reading Interest and Comprehension.* Ph.D. dissertation, Ohio State University, Columbus, 1971. (ED 067 625.)

BROWN, Kay Dian; KROCKOVER, Gerald H. A Reading Preference

Test: Rationale, Development, and Implementation, *Elementary English*, Vol. LI, No. 7, October 1974, p. 1003-4. (EJ 105 795.)

BRYANT, Antusa S.; BRYANT, Benjamin F. Some Considerations in Teaching Adults to Read, *Minnesota Reading Quarterly*, Vol. XVI, No. 1, October 1971, p. 11-14. (EJ 045 735.)

BURNET, Mary. *ABC of Literacy*. Paris, Unesco, 1965. (ED 022 122.)

BUTTS, Priscilla; SANDERS, June. *Motivated Reading: A Supervisor's Manual for a Tutorial Reading Program. Part 1: Information on Operating the Program*. Madison, Wis., University of Wisconsin, Research and Development Center for Cognitive Learning, 1972. (ED 073 445.)

BUTTZ, John Raymond. *Educational Goals and Motivational Determinants Inherent in Participants in Volunteer Literacy Education*. Ed.D. thesis, Indiana University, Bloomington, 1968. (ED 030 065.)

CARLSEN, G. Robert. The Interest Rate Is Rising. *English Journal*, Vol. LIX, No. 5, May 1970, p. 655-9. (EJ 019 513.)

COLLINS, Robert H. Books, Read Them and Keep Them. *Southern Education Report*, Vol. III, No. 5, December 1967. (ED 017 609.)

CORCORAN, Pat. The School for Thinking Is Worth Some Thought. *Reading Newsreport*, Vol. VI, No. 5, March 1972, p. 30-3. (EJ 065 588.)

COUVERT, R. Motivations of Malagasy Peasants. *Literacy Discussion*, Vol. II, No. 2, spring, 1971, p. 35-62. (EJ 038 831.)

CRISCUOLO, Nicholas P. A City Promotes a Reading Campaign. *New England Reading Association Journal*, Vol. VI, No. 2, spring, 1971, p. 23. (EJ 039 924.)

DAVIS, Bertha M. *et al*. Teaching Reading to the Bilingual Child: Motivational Techniques. *Sharing Ideas*, Vol. VII, No. 6, 1970. Phoenix, Arizona State Department of Education. (ED 055 698.)

DESJARDINS, Mary. Reading and Viewing: A Survey. *School Libraries*, Vol. XXI, No. 3, spring, 1972, p. 26-30. (EJ 054 047.)

DOBRYNINA, N. E.; STEL'MAH, V. D. Research on Reading and Readers' Interests in the U.S.S.R., *Unesco Bulletin for Libraries*, Vol. XXVII, No. 3, May-June 1973, p. 160-6, 183. (EJ 084 860.)

DONOHUE, Dan *et al. Guidelines for Teaching the Undereducated Adult*. Washington Office of the State Superintendent of Public Instruction, Olympia, 1966. (ED 012 411.)

DORAISWAMI, S. *Curriculum Preparation for Adult Education Programme—An Indian Experiment*. New Delhi, Ministry of Education and Social Welfare, 1974. (ED 110 675.)

EBERWEIN, Lowell. What Do Book Choices Indicate? *Journal of Reading*, Vol. XVII, No. 3, December 1973, p. 186–91. (EJ 087 639.)

EISENBERG, Leon. Reading Retardation: 1. Psychiatric and Sociologic Aspects. *Pediatrics*, Vol. XXXVII, No. 2, February 1966. (ED 034 651.)

ELVOVE, Marjorie R. Significant Trends in the Reading Habits of Senior High School Students. *English Record*, Vol. XXIII, No. 3, spring, 1973, p. 83–7. (EJ 076 744.)

ENNIS, Philip H. *Book Reading Audiences and the Mass Society*. Chicago, Ill., National Opinion Research Center, 1966. (ED 104 402.)

ESTES, Thomas H. A Scale to Measure Attitudes toward Reading. *Journal of Reading*, Vol. XV, No. 2, November 1971, p. 135–8. (EJ 046 711.)

ESTES, Thomas H.; VAUGHAN, Joseph L., Jr. Reading Interest and Comprehension: Implications, *Reading Teacher*, Vol. XXVII, No. 2, November 1973, p. 149–53. (EJ 085 861.)

FAIRLEIGH, Roberta *et al.* A Picture Inventory to Measure Children's Reading Interests. *Elementary English*, Vol. LI, No. 7, October 1974, p. 1011–12. (EJ 105 800.)

FAST, Elizabeth T. *The Media Program is an Integral Part of the Reading Program*. Groton, Conn., Groton Public Schools, March 1974. (ED 098 931.)

FEELEY, Joan T. Interest Patterns and Media Preferences of Middle-Grade Children. *Elementary English*, Vol. LI, No. 7, October 1974, p. 1006–8. (EJ 105 797.)

——. Television and Children's Reading. *Elementary English*, Vol. L, No. 1, January 1973, p. 141–8. (EJ 075 337.)

FENWICK, G. Junior School Pupils' Rejection of School Library Books. *Educational Research*, Vol. XVII, No. 2, February 1975, p. 143–9. (EJ 115 251.)

FITOURI, Chadly. An Experiment in Reading Motivation Techniques. *Prospects*, Vol. II, No. 2, summer, 1972, p. 206–13. (EJ 062 573.)

FLANIGAN, Michael. Reading Motivation; Needed: Some Indirection. *Viewpoints*, Vol. XLVIII, No. 1, January 1972, p. 57–63. (EJ 052 114.)

FLEITZ, Jeanette; HARMAN, Ronald. Free Reading Is a Simple Idea, but It Works. *Arizona English Bulletin*, Vol. XI, No. 3, April 1969, p. 6–8. (ED 032 302.)

FLEMING, James T. Relevance of Differential Thematic Content to Children's Self-selection of Reading Matter. *Elementary English*, Vol. XLVIII, No. 7, November 1971, p. 833–8. (EJ 047 935.)

Fox, Karen F.; Jung, Steven M. A Pilot Study of the Use of Incentives to Enhance School Learning. Paper presented at the annual meeting of the American Educational Research Association in Chicago, Ill., on 3–7 April 1972. Palo Alto, Calif., American Institutes for Research in the Behavioral Sciences, 1972. (ED 062 668.)

Freeman, Jayne. Learning to Love to Read. *Teacher*, Vol. XCII, No. 8, April 1975, p. 55–7, p. 117. (EJ 118 611.)

Freiberger, Rema. *The New York Times Report on Teenage Reading Tastes and Habits*. New York, N.Y., New York Times Co., 1974. (ED 092 868.)

Gates, Karen M. A Readmobile Takes to the Road, *Journal of Reading*, Vol. XIV, No. 2, November 1970, p. 89–93. (EJ 028 986.)

Geeslin, Dorine H.; Wilson, Richard C. Effect of Reading Age on Reading Interests. *Elementary English*, Vol. XLIX, No. 5, May 1972, p. 750–6. (EJ 058 236.)

Gotkin, Lassar G.; McSweeney, Joseph. *The Development of a Beginning Reading Skills Program Using the Edison Responsive Environments Instrument. Fourth Progress Report*. New York, N.Y., New York University School of Education, 1967. (ED 015 842.)

Granger, Virgie E. Yes, Virginia, They Can Learn to Read. Paper presented at the 26th annual meeting of the Conference on College Composition and Communication, St. Louis, Mo., 13–15 March 1975. (ED 103 873.)

Grant, Gloria W. *The Effect of Text Materials with Relevant Language, Illustrations and Content upon the Reading Achievement and Reading Preference (Attitude) of Black Primary and Intermediate Inner-City Students*. Ph.D. dissertation, University of Wisconsin, 1973. (ED 089 221.)

Grate, Donna D. Library Excursions Stimulate Awareness. *Indiana Reading Quarterly*, Vol. IV, No. 2, winter, 1972, p. 27, 31. (EJ 054 052.)

Grebelsky, Ora. *From Illiteracy to Literacy*. Jerusalem, Keter Publishing House, 1971. (ED 060 273.)

Greenberg, Marilyn Werstein. A Study of Reading Motivation of Twenty-three Seventh-Grade Students. *Library Quarterly*, Vol. XL, No. 3, July 1970, p. 309–17. (EJ 024 981.)

HALL, Budd L. (ed.). *The 1971 Literacy Campaign*. Dar es Salaam, Institute of Adult Education, Dar es Salaam University, 1971. (ED 058 560.)

HAMILTON, Harlan. Try TV Tie-ins. *Instructor*, Vol. LXXXIV, No. 8, April 1975, p. 67–9. (EJ 116 914.)

HAMILTON, Harlan Bernhardt. *The Relationship between Televiewing and the Reading Interests of Seventh Grade Pupils*. Ed.D. dissertation, Boston University School of Education, 1973. (ED 095 524.)

HARRIS, Albert J. New Dimensions in Basal Readers. *Reading Teacher*, Vol. XXV, No. 4, January 1972, p. 310–15. (EJ 049 486.)

HASKINS, Jack B.; FLYNNE, Lois P. Effect of Headline Typeface Variation on Reading Interest. *Journalism Quarterly*, Vol. LI, No. 4, winter, 1974, p. 677–82. (EJ 114 092.)

Holidays Can Make it Happen. *Reading Newsreport*, Vol. VI, No. 2, November–December 1971, p. 54–5. (EJ 049 901.)

HOLLINDALE, Peter. The Book That Does the Trick. *Times Educational Supplement*, London, 3 May 1974. (EJ 097 376.)

HOUSEMAN, Ann Lord. Tuned in to the Entire Family—A Book Festival. *Reading Teacher*, Vol. XXVII, No. 3, December 1973, p. 246–8. (EJ 087 622.)

HOVIOUS, Marilyn. Motivating Junior High Readers. *Journal of Reading*, Vol. XVII, No. 5, February 1974, p. 373–5. (EJ 091 154.)

HUDON, Sister Mary Oliver. *An Investigation of the Effectiveness of Two Motivational Techniques for Promoting Interest in Reading among Second Graders*. Ph.D. dissertation, University of Maryland, 1973. (ED 095 491.)

HUSSAIN, Ch. Ghulam. Pakistan: Motivating Adults for Learning. *Literacy Work*, Vol. III, No. 1, July 1973, p. 71–82. (EJ 087 367.)

INDIANA STATE DEPARTMENT OF PUBLIC INSTRUCTION. *Motivation and the Right to Read. Proceedings of a Conference Sponsored by the Indiana State Library and the Indiana Department of Public Instruction, Indianapolis, Ind., August 24–26, 1972*. (ED 073 774.)

INTERNATIONAL BUREAU OF EDUCATION. *Literacy and Education for Adults: 27th International Conference on Public Education, Geneva*. Paris, Unesco, 1964. (ED 021 169.)

INTERNATIONAL READING ASSOCIATION. UTAH COUNCIL. *Motivating Interest in Reading*. 1971. (ED 083 547.)

JAN-TAUSCH, Evelyn. Discovery and Measurement of Interests in Reading. *International Reading Association Conference Proceedings*, Part 4, 1968, p. 116–25. (EJ 019 288.)

JOHNS, Jerry L. What Do Inner-City Children Prefer to Read?

Reading Teacher. Vol. XXVI, No. 5, February 1973, p. 462–7. (EJ 073 679.)

JOHNS, Jerry L.; LUNT, Linda. Motivating Reading: Professional Ideas. *Reading Teacher*, Vol. XXVIII, No. 7, April 1975, p. 617–19. (EJ 115 681.)

JOHNSON, Lucetta A. A Multimedia Approach to Reading. *Reading Horizons*. Vol. X, No. 2, winter, 1970, p. 71–6. (EJ 015 141.)

JOHNSON, Simon S. How Students Feel about Literature. *American Education*, Vol. X, No. 3, April 1974, p. 6–10. (EJ 093 925.)

——. *A Survey of Reading Habits: Theme 4, Literature*. Denver, Colo., Education Commission of the States, National Assessment of Educational Progress, 1973. (ED 078 366.)

JOHNSON, Terry D. Must It Always Be the Three Little Pigs? *Reading Teacher*, Vol. XXIV, No. 3, December 1970, p. 209–15. (EJ 031 475.)

JOHNSON, William. Books for Sale. *Elementary English*, Vol. XLIX, No. 2, February 1972, p. 233–4. (EJ 052 429.)

JUSTIN, Neal. Mexican-American Reading Habits and Their Cultural Basis. *Journal of Reading*, Vol. XVI, No. 6, March 1973, p. 467–73. (EJ 075 159.)

KIMBROUGH, James Daniel. *A Study of the Recreational Reading of Fourth, Fifth, and Sixth Grade Children*. Ed.D. dissertation, University of Alabama, 1972. (ED 079 679.)

KIMMEL, Eric Alan. *Children's Reading and Attitude Change*. Ph.D. dissertation, University of Illinois, Urbana-Champaign, 1973. (ED 082 165.)

KINGSTON, Albert J. A Hierarchy of Reading Behaviors. Paper presented at the National Reading Conference, Atlanta, Ga., 4–6 December 1969. (ED 036 416.)

KINNAMON, Sue. Commercial Television and Adult Reading. *Journal of Reading*, Vol. XVIII, No. 6, March 1975, p. 470–4. (EJ 112 372.)

KIRSCH, Dorothy I. *Current Expressed Reading Interests of Young Children*. Ed.D. dissertation, Hofstra University, Hempstead, N.Y., 1973. (ED 090 488.)

——. From Athletes to Zebras—Young Children Want to Read about Them. *Elementary English*, Vol. LII, No. 1, January 1975, p. 73–8. (EJ 110 865.)

——. What about Reading 'Interests' in the Open Classroom? Paper presented at the 19th Annual Meeting of the International Reading Association, New Orleans, La., 1–4 May 1974. (ED 089 218.)

KIRSHNER, A. J. A Cause of Poor Reading Is Poor Reading. *Special Education in Canada*, Vol. XLVII, No. 3, April 1973, p. 13–19, 22–5. (EJ 091 350.)

KIT CARSON UNION ELEMENTARY SCHOOL DISTRICT. HANFORD, CALI-FORNIA. *Motivation for Reading Improvement: Final Project Report*. Sacramento, California State Department of Education, 1973. (ED 096 622.)

KOLCZYNSKI, Richard. Boy's Right to Read: Sexuality Factors in Learning to Read. Paper presented at the 18th Annual Meeting of the International Reading Association, Denver, Colo., 1–4 May 1973. (ED 078 389.)

LEESON, Jeanne Tellier. Short Fiction Motivated Upper-Grade Reading. *Instructor*, Vol. LXXVIII, No. 8, p. 70–2. (EJ 003 115.)

LIAN-HWAN CHIU. Reading Preferences of Fourth Grade Children Related to Sex and Reading Ability. *Journal of Educational Research*, Vol. LXVI, No. 8, April 1973, p. 369–73. (EJ 075 703.)

LOHRER, Alice (ed.). *Research in the Fields of Reading and Com-munications*. Urbana, Ill., University of Illinois Press, 1973. (ED 085 690.)

LONG, Barbara H.; HENDERSON, Edmund H. *Children's Use of Time: Some Personal and Social Correlations*. Goucher College, Balti-more, Md.; Virginia University, Charlottesville, Va., 1970. (ED 054 475.)

LOWE, A. J. The Rise of College Reading: the Good, the Bad, and the Indifferent: 1915–1970. Paper presented to the College Reading Association convention, Philadelphia, Pa., 19–21 March 1970. (ED 040 013.)

LOWTHER, Barbara Doty. *The Effects of Verbal and Monetary Incen-tives on Reading in Adult Illiterates. Final Report*. Naperville, Ill., North Central College, 1973. (ED 080 974.)

LYMAN, Helen H. *Library Materials in Service to the Adult New Reader: Phase I, The Planning Year First Report*. Madison, Wis., University of Wisconsin Library School, 1968. (ED 024 436.)

McCONKIE, George W. *et al*. Experimental Manipulation of Reading Strategies. *Journal of Educational Psychology*, Vol. LXV, No. 1, August 1973, p. 1–8. (EJ 083 570.)

McCROSSAN, John. *The Reading of the Culturally Disadvantaged*. Urbana, Ill., University of Illinois, 1966. (ED 010 755.)

McNINCH, George. Determining the Reading Preferences of Third, Fourth, and Fifth Grade Disadvantaged Pupils. *Journal of Reading Behavior*, Vol. III, No. 2, spring, 1970–71, p. 32–8. (EJ 045 397.)

MAITRA, Satyen. Organisational and Motivational Problems in Adult Literacy Programmes. *Indian Journal of Adult Education*, Vol. XXXI, No. 7, July 1970, p. 5–8, 19–20. (EJ 028 941.)

MARTADIDJAJA, P. S. A New Approach to Adult Literacy in Indonesia. *Indian Journal of Adult Education*, Vol. XXXII, No. 10, October 1971, p. 7–9. (EJ 061 111.)

MARTIN, Robert E. Too Much Teaching; Too Little Reading. *Education Digest*, Vol. XXXV, No. 1, September 1969, p. 38–40. (EJ 008 372.)

MARTIN, Robert Lee. *Interestability of Sixth Grade Basic Readers*. Ed.D. dissertation, University of Southern California, Los Angeles, 1972. (ED 065 857.)

MAXWELL, Martha J., MUELLER, Arthur C. *An Experiment on the Effect of Motivational Appeals vs. Techniques upon Reading Rate Improvement in a Group of College Students*. College Park, Md., University of Maryland, 1965. (ED 011 490.)

MEADE, Edward J., Jr. Reading: The First 'R'—a Point of View. *Reading World*, Vol. XII, No. 3, March 1973, p. 169–80. (EJ 073 768.)

MERLA, Patrick. 'What Is Real?' Asked the Rabbit One Day. *Saturday Review: The Arts*, Vol. LV, No. 45, 4 November 1972, p. 43–50. (EJ 067 177.)

MINISTRY OF EDUCATION AND SOCIAL WELFARE, NEW DELHI. *Handbook on Farmers' Functional Literacy Project*. New Delhi, 1971. (ED 060 432.)

MORRISON, Donald W. The Effects on Anxiety and Verbal Motivational Approaches on the Reading Performance of Children. *Reading Improvement*, Vol. XI, No. 2, February 1974, p. 26–31. (EJ 103 975.)

NARANG, H. L. Materials for College and Adult Reading Improvement Programs. *Reading World*, Vol. XII, No. 3, March 1973, p. 181–8. (EJ 073 591.)

NATIONAL BOOK COMMITTEE, INC. *International Book Year 1972: A Handbook for U.S. Participation*. New York, N.Y., 1971. (ED 059 725.)

——. *Sound and Light for the Right to Read*. New York, N.Y., 1971. (ED 094 355.)

NATIONAL READING CENTER FOUNDATION. *Adult Reading Development: An Information Awareness Service*. Washington, D.C. (ED 059 482.)

NEW YORK STATE EDUCATION DEPARTMENT. *A New Motivation for*

Learning: The Graphics Expression System. Manual for Admin-istrators. Albany, N.Y., Albany Division of Educational Com-munications, 1973. (ED 079 965.)

NORVELL, George W. Revolution in the English Curriculum, *Elementary English*, Vol. XLIX, No. 5, May 1972, p. 760–7. (EJ 057 219.)

ODOKARA, E. O. Innovative Practices in East Central State, *Adult Education* (Lond.), Vol. XLV, No. 1, May 1972, p. 32–7. (EJ 060 064.)

O'DONNELL, Holly. ERIC/RCS: Student Reading Interests. *Journal of Reading*, Vol. XVII, No. 2, November 1973, p. 168–9. (EJ 085 887.)

PAISLEY, William, J.; REES, Matilda B. Social and Psychological Predictors of Information Seeking and Media Use. A Multi-variate Re-analysis. Paper presented at the National Seminar on Adult Education Research, Chicago, Ill., 11–13 February 1968. (ED 017 819.)

PENROSE, Jeanne *et al.* The Newspaper Nonreader 10 Years Later: A Partial Replication of Westley-Severin. *Journalism Quarterly*, Vol. LI, No. 4, winter, 1974, p. 631–8. (EJ 114 084.)

PETRE, Richard M. Reading Breaks Make It in Maryland. *Journal of Reading*, Vol. XV, No. 3, December 1971, p. 491–4. (EJ 051 101.)

PHILLIPS, H. M. *Literacy and Development*, Paris, Unesco, 1970. (ED 045 882.)

POTEET, G. H. A High School Read-in, *Reading Improvement*, Vol. VIII, No. 1, spring, 1971, p. 21–2. (EJ 038 491.)

RAMOS, Marcos S. The Role of the Schools in the Promotion of Adult Literacy. *ASPBAE Journal*, Vol. III, Nos. 2–3, November 1968–February 1969, p. 27–37. (EJ 009 930.)

RESNICK, Lauren B.; ROBINSON, Betty H. *Motivational Aspects of the Literacy Problem.* Pittsburgh, Pa., University of Pittsburgh, Learning Research and Development Center, 1971. (ED 099 799.)

ROBINSON, H. Alan *et al.* Expressed Reading Interests of Young Children: An International Study. Paper presented at the 5th International Reading Association World Congress on Reading, Vienna, Austria, 12–14 August 1974. (ED 096 614.)

ROEDER, Harold H.; LEE, Nancy. Twenty-five Teacher-Tested Ways to Encourage Voluntary Reading. *Reading Teacher*, Vol. XXVII, No. 1, October 1973, p. 48–50. (EJ 084 350.)

ROMANI, Dorothy. Reading Interests and Needs of Older People. *Library Trends*, Vol. XXI, No. 3, January 1973, p. 390–403. (EJ 078 437.)

ROSE, Cynthia *et al*. Content Counts: Children Have Preferences in Reading Textbook Stories. *Elementary English*, Vol. XLIX, No. 1, January 1972, p. 14–19. (EJ 049 493.)

SAINT LOUIS BOARD OF EDUCATION. *Report for the First Year of a Project to Provide New Motivation for Reading through Library Services in Overcrowded Elementary Schools*, Saint Louis, Mo., 1968. (ED 024 545.)

SAULS, Charles. The Relationship of Selected Factors to Recreational Reading of Sixth Graders. *Elementary English*, Vol. LI, No. 7, October 1974, p. 1009–11. (EJ 105 799.)

SCHARF, Anne G. Who Likes What in High School? *Journal of Reading*, Vol. XVI, No. 8, May 1973, p. 604–7. (EJ 077 322.)

SCHULTE, Emerita Schroer. Independent Reading Interests of Children in Grades Four, Five, and Six. *International Reading Association Conference Proceedings*, Part I, Vol. 13, April 1968, p. 728–32. (EJ 019 189.)

——. Today's Literature for Today's Children. *Elementary English*, Vol. XLIX, No. 3, March 1972, p. 355–63. (EJ 056 099.)

SHARON, Amiel T. What Do Adults Read? *Reading Research Quarterly*, Vol. IX, No. 2, 1973–74, p. 148–69. (EJ 092 583.)

SHIRLEY, Fehl L. Case Studies of the Influence of Reading on Adolescents. *Research in the Teaching of English*, Vol. III, No. 1, spring, 1969, p. 30–41. (EJ 005 779.)

SHNAYER, Sidney W. Relationships between Reading Interest and Reading Comprehension. *International Reading Association Conference Proceedings*, Part I, Vol. 13, April 1968, p. 698–702. (EJ 019 184.)

SHORTRIDGE, Cleona B. Creating an Environment for the Teaching of Reading. Paper presented at the 19th Annual Meeting of the International Reading Association, New Orleans, La., 1–4 May 1974. (ED 094 370.)

SINGH, Jane M. Research in Homework as the Motivating Factor in Reading Achievement. *Journal of Reading Behaviour*, Vol. III, No. 3, summer, 1971, p. 51–60. (EJ 049 004.)

SMITH, James L. Motivating the Illiterate Adult. *Adult Leadership*, Vol. XXIII, No. 11, May 1975, p. 342–4. (EJ 118 800.)

SMITH, J. R.; JOHNSON, F. N. The Popularity of Children's Fiction as a Function of Reading Ease and Related Factors. *Journal of Educational Research*, Vol. LXV, No. 9, May–June 1972, p. 397–400. (EJ 061 108.)

SMITH, Marshall S. (ed.). *Attention and Motivation, Panel 3: Conference on Studies in Reading.* Washington, D.C., National Institute of Education (DHEW), July 1975.

SMITH, Marshall S. (ed.). *Learning and Motivation in Early Reading, Panel 8: Conference on Studies in Reading.* Washington, D.C., National Institute of Education (DHEW), August 1975. (ED 112 392.)

SOLOMON, Bernard. To Achieve, Not to Please. *Learning Today,* Vol. VIII, No. 1, winter, 1975, p. 48–51. (EJ 111 359.)

SONI, Dayal Chandra. Ghandian Basic Education as Applied to Adult Literacy. *Indian Journal of Adult Education,* Vol. XXXV, No. 2, February 1974, p. 3–11. (EJ 102 156.)

SORENSON, Juanita S. *et al. The Individual Conference—A Motivational Device for Increasing Independent Reading in the Elementary Grades.* Madison, Wis., University of Wisconsin, Research and Development Center for Cognitive Learning, 1969. (ED 039 110.)

SQUIRE, James R. What Does Research in Reading Reveal—about Attitudes toward Reading? *English Journal,* Vol. LVIII, No. 4, April 1969, p. 523–33. (EJ 004 950.)

STEMMLER, Anne O. Reading of Highly Creative versus Highly Intelligent Secondary Students. Paper presented at International Reading Association Conference, Boston, Mass., 24–7 April 1968. (ED 028 027.)

TAYLOR, J. J. The Voluntary Book Reading Habits of Secondary School Pupils, *Use of English,* Vol. XXV, No. 1, autumn, 1973, p. 5–12, 16. (EJ 100 799.)

TRISMEN, Donald A. Adult Readers: Activities and Goals. Paper presented at the meeting of the American Educational Research Association, Chicago, Ill., April 1972. (ED 061 024.)

——. Targeted Research and Development Program in Reading—The Search for Criteria. Paper presented at the meeting of the American Educational Research Association, New York, N.Y., 4–7 February 1971. (ED 050 894.)

TRUE, Judith N. *A Comparison of Reading Interests by Economic Levels.* Ph.D. dissertation, Georgia State University School of Education, 1974. (ED 105 399.)

TUSKEGEE INSTITUTE. *Experiment in Motivating Functional Illiterates to Learn. Final Report.* Alabama School of Applied Sciences, 1969. (ED 039 442.)

UNESCO. *Books for All, a Programme of Action.* Paris, 1973. (ED 091 008.)

——. *Study Visit and Seminar: Work-oriented Adult Literacy Pilot Project in Iran. Final Report.* Paris, 1970. (ED 048 564.)

VANDER MEULEN, Kenneth. Teaching Reading in the Secondary
School: 'The Fine Art of Motivation'. *Reading Horizons*,
Vol. XIII, No. 2, winter, 1973, p. 84–8. (EJ 070 044.)

VAUGHN, Susan. Monster Movies? *School Library Journal*,
October 1971, p. 83–5. (EJ 046 313.)

VEERARAGHAVAN, J. Motivation and Adult Education, *Indian Journal
of Adult Education*, Vol. XXXV, Nos. 4–5, April–May 1974,
p. 18–21. (EJ 102 231.)

VERI, Clive C. *A Bill of Rights for Functionally Illiterate Adults.*
(ED 078 274.)

VIZCONDE, A. C. Adult Education in the Philippines. *Indian Journal
of Adult Education*, Vol. XXXII, No. 12, December 1971,
p. 13–16. (EJ 054 337.)

WARSH, H. E. *Behavior Modification of Adult Illiterates and Functional
Illiterates Who Learned to Read*. Ed.D. thesis, Wayne State University, Detroit, Mich., 1969. (ED 048 532.)

WASHOE COUNTY SCHOOL DISTRICT. *Mobile Diagnostic Van, End of
Project Year Report*, Nevada, 1973. (ED 096 621.)

WEBER, Vannette. Special Folders for Reading Aids. *Pointer*, Vol. XIX,
No. 2, winter, 1974, p. 111–12. (EJ 112 529.)

WEINTRAUB, Samuel. Children's Reading Interests. *Reading Teacher*,
Vol. XXII, No. 7, April 1969, p. 655, 657, 659. (EJ 003 155.)

WHEATCROFT, Les. *Something for Nothing: An Experimental Book
Exposure Programme*. Peterborough, Ontario, CANLIT, 1975.
(ED 112 403.)

WHEELER, A. H. Motivation for Wide Reading: An Individualized
Reading Program. *New England Reading Association Journal*,
Vol. V, No. 2, winter, 1970, p. 22–7. (EJ 016 505.)

WILLERMAN, Marvin; WILLERMAN, Barbara. Effects of Motivational Conferences. *Journal of Reading*, Vol. XVII, No. 3,
December 1973, p. 224–7. (EJ 087 647.)

WINEBRENNER, Rosemary. *How Can I Get My Teenager to Read?*
Bloomington, Ind., Indiana University, 1971. (ED 057 988.)

*World Literacy and Christian Literature. Report on an Experimental
Study of an Intensive Five-Week Literacy-Homecraft Course.
Conducted at Women's Seminar, Singida, Tanzania, July 13–
August 14, 1970*. New York, N.Y., 1970. (ED 059 451.)

ZIMET, Sara G.; CAMP, Bonnie W. A Comparison Between the Content
of Preferred School Library Book Selections Made by Inner-
City and Suburban First Grade Students. *Elementary English*,
Vol. LI, No. 7, October 1974, p. 1004–6. (EJ 105 796.)